100 MOST IMPORTANT HOME IMPROVEMENT TIPS

How to buy, sell, improve & take care of your home

Glenn Haege

Edited by Kathy Stief
Cover Photo by David Frechette
Back Cover Photo by Ewald Stief

MASTER HANDYMAN PRESS, INC.

100 MOST IMPORTANT HOME IMPROVEMENT TIPS
How to buy, sell, improve & take care of your home

Glenn Haege

Edited by Kathy Stief

Published by:
> Master Handyman Press, Inc.
> Post Office Box 1498
> Royal Oak, MI 48068-1498 USA

First Printing February 2004

Printed in the United States of America

Library of Congress Cataloging in Publication Data.
Haege, Glenn
> Upgrading and maintaining your home
> Bibliography: h.

ISBN 1-880615-89-4

*To Diane Bliss at Detroit, Public Television,
for insisting that I get this book done in time for the
biggest fundraising period of the year.*

*To Doug Beauvais, Data Reproductions Corp.,
for making the book a reality*

Acknowledgments

My staff and I have been working on this book for three years but all of a sudden we were committed to a public television fundraising special and an "always on the back burner" project became an almost impossible rush.

All the folks at Master Handyman Press put in super long hours. Kathy and Ewald Stief, my editor and research editor / publisher did much of the digging and fine-tuning. Kelly Boike and her mother, Barbara Anderson, double and triple-checked all the phone numbers and waded through countless files. Rob David, my marketing director, Pat Sheehan my affiliate relations director, and my radio show producer, Dave "King Pin" Riger, did yeoman service tracking down obscure web sites and phone numbers. Deborah Ciavattone came in at the last moment and magically turned a MicroSoft Word manuscript into Page Maker files with one hand while proofreading and designing with the other. Doug Beauvais at Data Reproductions twisted arms and pulled a book out of thin air.

All the folks at Detroit Public Television deserve a round of applause for their help on the PBS special and video. Most especially I want to thank Diane Bliss, Jeff Forster, Amy Zielinski, Karyn Hertel, Josette Marano (who can make something out of nothing), Charles Mercado (who can make it look good), Anne (his mother), Jaime Jendzejewski, Aimee Longato, Jocelyn Dotson, my co-stars Damon Creighton, Jackqueline Jerore and Ron Jendzejewski, and Jayne Laube-Nelson and her magical makeup kit, as well as the entire production crew of very hard working people.

In between writing books and doing television my "real job" is host of the nation's only 7-day a week how to talk show. The Handyman Show with Glenn Haege runs on WXDX - 1310 - Detroit, Monday - Friday, and WDFN - 1130 - Detroit, Saturdays and Sundays and is syndicated nationally by Handyman Productions, LLC. Just call 1 (866) ASK-GLENN.

A book like this could not be written without input from many technical experts. There are so many of them that I know I will miss many great folks, but here are just a few: Angelo Zerbo and Pat Solar, A & Z Roofing; Karen Collins, Broan-Nutone; Brian Burke, Burke Agency; Don Collins, Budget Electric; Mike McCoy, Coy Construction; Sandy Cornillie, J. C. Cornillie; Bill Damman, Damman Hardware; Ray Kennedy Jr., Delta Faucet; Mike Shorkey, Detroit Safety Furnace; Dick Walters, Erickson Floor Supply; Gary Marowske, Flame Furnace; Adam Helfman, Fairway Construction, Steve Klochko, Gibraltar National; Mark Ratliff, Hartford & Ratliff; Jim Frensley, Hansen Marketing Services; Gabe Farkas, Icynene; Doug Dailey, Indoor Air Quality Distributors; Kim Craig-Boos, KraftMaid Cabinetry; Howard Kuretzky, Wayne Weintraub and Bob O'Brien, Kurtis Kitchen and Bath Centers; Samuel Cypert and Nan Schofner, Masco Corp.; Scott Ainsley, Lennox; Larry Wilson, Merillat Industries; Murray Gula, Michigan Construction Protection Agency; Pat Murphy, Pat Murphy, Inc.; George Chrenka and Steve Earley, Nu-Wool; David T. Brown, Wayne T. Power, Frank S. Tyler, Merle F. McBride, Donn Vermilion, Charles F. Pratt and Frank O'Brien-Bernini, Owens Corning; Joe Aiello, Pine Building; Bob Martin, Reddi-Wall; Mike Palazzolo, Safety King; Connie and Tom Morbach, Sanit-Air; Dave Felker, Sterling Enviornmental; Jim Kronk, Universal Plumbing; and old reliables, always there with all the facts, Jim Williams, Williams Refrigeration and Jimmy Kogut, Xavier Corporation.

Last of all are the most important people on my list: My wife, Barbara, who puts up with me and proofreads all my books, my kids, Eric and his wife Julie, and their son Mathew, and Heather and her husband Ray, and their daughters, Emily and Macy, and my mom, Marion.

Glenn Haege
Royal Oak, Michigan

Table of Contents

Chapter II   Major Projects   **49**

Chapter III   Major Home Systems   **109**

Heating, Cooling, Ventilation and Air Quality

Roofing, Insulation and Roof Venting

Chapter IV   Security   159

Chapter V   Plumbing & Electrical   177

Chapter VI   Emergencies   213

WARNING - DISCLAIMER

This book is designed to provide information for the home handy man and woman. It is sold with the understanding that the publisher and author are not engaged in rendering legal, contractor, architectural, or other professional services. If expert assistance is required, the services of competent professionals should be sought.

Every effort has been made to make this text as complete and accurate as possible, and to assure proper credit is given to various contributors and manufacturers, etc. However, there may be mistakes, both typographical and in content. Therefore, this text should be used only as a general guide and not as the ultimate source of information. Furthermore this book contains information only up to the printing date.

The purpose of this book is to educate and entertain. The author and Master Handyman Press shall have neither liability nor responsibility to any person or entity with respect to any loss or damage caused directly or indirectly by the information contained in this book.

WARNING - DISCLAIMER

Introduction

This is the first of three books I decided to write to celebrate my first 20 years hosting the Handyman Show. The other two books in the series are *One Hundred Most Important Painting Tips* and *One Hundred Most Important Cleaning Tips*.

Because of other projects the book is about eight months late, but Ewald tells me that somehow the other two will be out before my 21st anniversary next spring. Since I would not have gotten nearly this far if hard working optimists did not surround me, I believe him.

The book would have been a lot easier to write if it had been the "300 most important Home Improvement tips". We had almost 300 tips laid out 18 months ago. The problems are in the words "100" and "most important". I have tried to distill the most important information you need as the CEO of your single most important investment, your home.

For this reason this book is not a "How To" book in the usual sense of the word. I concentrate on the big picture instead of sweating the small stuff. I rather save you from making a $1,000 mistake than save $75 on a service call.

The step-by-step directions I give are for projects that are either so common you have to do them frequently or so critically important that you have to do the job immediately.

For those who want a more "hands on" approach, just wait for the second and third books in this series. I will give you more than enough information to keep you scrubbing, cleaning, prepping, painting and protecting your home 24 hours a day. Until then . . .

Enjoy the read.

Trademark Acknowledgments

Trademarked names, rather than confusion inducing, generic names, are used throughout this book so that readers can ask distributors, retailers, and contractors, about products that interest them. Rather than list the names and entities that own each trademark or insert a trademark symbol with each mention of the trademarked name, the publisher states that it is using the names only for editorial purposes and to the benefit of the trademark owner with no intent of infringing upon that trademark.

Trademark Acknowledgments

Chapter I
Buy or Remodel?

1 How to decide whether to move or improve

Your house was fine when you bought it. But then the kids came or your interests or job changed. Now your home is no longer convenient. It is old and you want new. It is cramped and you need extra room. What should you do?

Be very hard headed about your decision but do not jump to conclusions. A new home filled with the creature comforts you long for can still be a losing proposition. I have known many people who moved to the new and wonderful only to return to the old neighborhood in a couple of years and pay more money for less house than when they started their adventure.

In this very impersonal, stress filled age, established friendships, neighbors you can rely on, good schools that your kids like, your children's friends, your church, familiar stores, libraries and traffic patterns all spell quality of life. All should be given a cash value when considering a move.

If you like everything about your house, except your house, go house hunting. Find exactly what the home of your dreams in just the right neighborhood costs and also determine the value of your present house.

Catalogue everything that is wrong with your present house and what it would take to make it the house of your dreams. Call in the contractors and get estimates. Subtract the quality of life value of your present home from the cost of making it come up to your expectations.

Now compare the value of your current modified house to the house you are considering in the new neighborhood. If your present house looks like a better value, stay put and improve. If your new place now looks like a bargain, move.

Here's an example. You love the neighborhood, the schools, everything about the house except the house. It needs a $175,000 remodeling job. But you say that staying in that location is worth $75,000 to you and the rest of the family. A house with everything you want costs $450,000.

New House: $450,000
Present house
Market value: $300,000
+ Remodeling: $175,000   = $475,000
- Lifestyle value: $ 75,000   = $400,000

You're a winner staying where you are.

On the other hand if you hate the neighbors, are afraid the kids are going to start running with gangs and desperately want them to have better schools, the lifestyle value would go into negative territory. That equation might look like this:

New House: $450,000
Present house
Market value: $300,000
+ Remodeling: $175,000   = $475,000
+ Neg. Lifestyle: $100,000   = $575,000

This means that staying in your present home would actually cost you $125,000 more than the new house. It is time to call the mover.

2 How to fix up your house for resale

It is best to keep a running tally of what would be needed to get it ready for resale at all times. Then bite the bullet and do now, what you will eventually have to do anyway. This way you get to live with and enjoy the necessary improvements instead of living with the problems and fixing them for the other guy.

When it comes time to sell, fix or enhance the obvious. List the negatives and get quotes on needed repairs. Be scrupulously honest.

In many states honesty about home problems is not just a virtue, it is the law. If you pull a fast one on the new buyer, chances are that he will be able to sue, make you pay top dollar for needed repairs, and the state may even bring criminal charges. Not nice.

The things that make the biggest impression in order of importance are the following:
- √ The exterior of the house and grounds, especially the front, including the roof
- √ Paint
- √ Kitchen and Bath
- √ Carpeting

No matter how great a house you have, unless it looks good when the perspective buyers drive up to the curb, the sale is dead. Usually they won't even bother to get out of the car. That's why we say that curb appeal is up to 70% of the sale.

The roof is especially important if you have a ranch type house. If the shingles look worn, re-roof. If possible use dimensional shingles. They cost more but add a great deal of sales appeal to the house. If this is financially impossible, get an estimate for both standard and dimensional shingles.

When you or the sales person talks to shoppers, be positive. The house was going to be re-roofed, but the sellers thought it would be better if the new owners got just what they wanted. "Here is a quote. We will credit the price of standard shingles from the selling price."

Getting the rest of the exterior in shape is fairly easy. Make certain that the landscaping is up to snuff. If not, put in annuals. The grass should be well fertilized, watered and cut.

Give siding and trim a fresh coat of paint. Don't be creative. Use standard colors. The same thing holds true for the doors. The paint should be fresh and hardware should be shined within an inch of its life. Naturally windows should be sparkling.

When a house hunter steps inside a house, it should look and smell clean and be organized. If the paint is dingy, now is the perfect time to paint. If the house is cluttered, and most of our homes are cluttered, sweet talk some friends into letting you store some of your excess or worn furniture in their garage.

The kitchen and bath are the heart and lungs of the home. The wife makes a beeline to the kitchen and the husband goes straight to the bath, or visa-versa. No matter in what great shape the rest of the house and grounds are, if the kitchen and bath look bad, the house is a "fixer-upper".

If your kitchen and bath look out-dated now, shame on you. You should have had them up-dated every 10 or 12 years. That way you would have been happier with your house and the house would have been more valuable to perspective buyers. If most of your kitchen looks beautiful but you need new countertops, consider getting new countertops.

If you need new flooring and cabinetry, consider getting quotes so that your sales agent has something authoritative to hold in her hand when she discusses the kitchen. It is very easy for a buyer to look at an old kitchen and say that updating it will cost $30,000 to $50,000. If the real estate agent has your quotes, she can say "the flooring and appliances are almost new and according to this estimate replacing the cabinets and countertops will only cost $15,000". With luck, she might be able to turn a negative into a positive.

Whether you are going to make major modifications or not, any time and energy you spend making the kitchen and bath look their best will pay big dividends.

3 How to decide whether to do a job yourself or hire a contractor

Do It Yourself or Hire It Done is a major question when remodeling. The simple answer is the following. If you have the time, energy and desire to do the job and the results will be as good or better than if they were done by a professional, do it yourself. If the sales agent is going to have to make excuses for the "handyman" look, hire a professional.

How to projects are not brain surgery. If you are willing to take the time and have the talent, you can paint, stain and drywall with the best of them. You can even lay laminated flooring and install cabinets and windows. But understand this. If you do a bad job, you will wind up paying twice. Once when you do the work, and when your house is sold.

**Your house is your most important investment.
Do it right or have someone else do it.**

4 How to find a good remodeling contractor

There are three good ways to find a contractor.

1. **Ask your family, friends, and neighbors** who have had the same type of work done for them. If they were happy, the chances are very good that you will be also.

2. **Look in your neighborhood** for contractors doing the same type of work. If it looks like they are doing a good job and the homeowner is pleased, they would probably do a good job for you too. You can see how neat they keep the job site and the quality of their performance. You also know that they work in your neighborhood.

3. **Ask the folks who sell them their materials.** They know how the contractor pays his bills, how busy he is, whether he has a good work ethic.

If you want a good roofer, go to a roofing wholesale supply company. If you want a good tile man, go to one of the local tile wholesale distributors. Same thing for kitchen remodeling, paint, pavers, decks, you name it. Go to the contractor desk, explain what you want done, and ask for two or three names they would recommend.

When you get the names, call the contractors for appointments, let them know that you are in the loop. Say, John from Siding World recommended you for my siding job. That way they know who recommended them and, most importantly, that you know John. It makes a difference.

If you want a heating or cooling contractor, you may want to go to the web site of the manufacturer and see who they list as "elite" or "gold star" dealers. Most manufacturers list the contractors that have special qualifications.

No matter how you get the contractor's name, check his references before you give him the job.

5 How long a remodeling job should take

It may take us years to decide that we want a remodeling job done, but once we've made the decision we want it done yesterday. Most homeowners do not realize how long a remodeling job will take. Most contractors do not give them the information they need to get an honest appraisal of the task at hand. Unrealistic homeowner attitudes are a key cause for homeowner compliant.

If you have never done a major modernization before, there is no way for you to know how long it will take. Most builders don't want to tell you because they are afraid that you will go to some-

one else if they are honest.

A big job can easily take between 3-1/2 to 9 months between the time you start working with a salesman/designer seriously and the day the job is done. Luckily, most of these steps take place behind the scenes so your house is not torn up.

Some steps in the procedure take very little time. Some, like getting a Building Permit or requesting changes to existing ordinances can easily take 30 to 60 days.

Here's a chart to tell you the steps in the remodeling procedure. Most of these names are self-explanatory. I go into great detail on this in my book, *Fix It Fast & Easy! 2, Upgrading Your House*. The "Hand Off Meeting" is the day in which you meet with the salesman/designer and the key members of the actual construction team, like the building superintendent and lead carpenter. The reason that this can take up to 7 days is that getting all these busy people together for the meeting is a miracle.

Major Remodeling Time Frame

Task	# Days Minimum	Maximum
Meeting with Salesman/ Designer	1	1
Days to final plan	7	14
Blue prints from architect	7	28
Request for Building Permit	14	30
Variances or Change plan to Conform to Code	0	60
Hand off meeting	1	7
Special Orders	28	42
Time to Start Date	35	56
Actual construction	14	35
Total Days	**107**	**273**

6 How to make sure the contractor completes the job on time

Many builders will tell you, "We'll start your job right away." Actually, you don't care when the job starts, you only care when it will be finished. The best way to do this is to make sure that the completion date is written into the contract.

Contractors hate it when I tell homeowners to do this. They don't want to be pinned down and would like to be able to postpone completion of your job if other projects creep up.

Philosophically you are, I am sure, a very compassionate person. But if your house and your family's life has been torn apart for two or three weeks, you don't really give a darn about your builder's problems. You want the job done when promised.

Put in a completion date and give it muscle with a "reward and penalty" clause on larger jobs.

The contractor should get $X per day more for every day he is done early and have to deduct $X per day from the total invoice for every day he is late completing the job.

7 What to include in the remodeling contract

When you and the salesman or contractor agree on a deal, he will usually pull out a "standard" contract and start filling it in. If you tell him that you want to make changes, he may look at you as if you are trying to change holy writ. Don't be bamboozled. There is no such thing as an industry standard unless it is something concocted by association lawyers to make an agreement that is entirely in the contractor's favor.

Here is a breakdown of the minimum information the contract should hold, as well as the reason you want the information. If the contractor does not want that information included in the contract, you do not want the contractor working on your house.

The name, address, phone number, and builder's license number of both the contracting company and the person who actually holds the license.

In the event of a problem, you want to know who is really responsible for doing the work and who your lawyer will have to go after, because they are the legally responsible party. This can be two completely different parties.

Quite often a retired or out-of-business licensed builder will rent his or her license to a contractor who has either lost his license or never been good enough to pass the licensing exam. The licensee's only connection to your job may be that he or she signs the required permit applications. If something goes wrong, the contractor who actually botched the job can wash his hands of the matter, and you will have to sue the license holder who may not have any assets. It is vitally important for you to know this before signing a contract.

An exact description of what is going to be done with the work broken down by value.

If the contractor is asking for staged payments, you want to know how much will have to be paid for each step of the way. You also want to know the approximate value of work in case you have disagreements about costs while the job is being completed.

An exact description of all major materials, such as windows or roofing, by manufacturer, brand name and model number.

You can expect one thing and get another. If you have it in writing and don't get it, you can make the contractor replace the materials. If you don't have it in writing, you can't.

A listing of every trade contractor who will be on your job site, along with licensing information, telephone numbers and insurance information.

If something goes wrong and your job superintendent is not getting the problem solved, you want to be able to go directly to the source and find out the real reason for the problem.

A promise to provide you with signed waivers of lien forms by the trades in exchange for payment.

If the contractor does not pay his suppliers or sub contractors, they have the right to lien your property. It doesn't matter if you paid the contractor, you can be required to pay twice. If you have a waiver of lien form stating that the required payments have been made, they can't lien you and your property is safe.

A promise to provide you with copies of all guaranties and warranties on all materials and equipment that is being used on the job.

Two or three years from now something can go wrong that should be under warranty. The builder may have gone off into the sunset or be completely uninterested about helping you solve your problem. The only way you can get satisfaction is if you have a copy of the required warranty.

A promise that the contractor's insurance company, not the contractor, will provide you with a certificate of insurance.

Your contractor's policy could have been canceled a month ago. The only way you can make certain that the contractor is truly covered for workmen's compensation and liability insurance is if his insurance carriers or their agents send you certificates of insurance directly.

Start and completion dates with reward and penalty clauses citing actual daily amounts that you or the contractor will be required to pay if the job is completed early or late.

You want to give the contractor an incentive to get the work done fast. You want to also give him a very big reason to finish the job on time.

A description of whom is responsible for clean up and when it will be done. There should also be a description of who owns the materials left on the job site.

Clean up often becomes a hassle. The contractor says you have to do it. You say the contractor is supposed to do it. Also many people feel that they bought all the materials delivered to a job site. This is often not the case. Many good contractors ship more to the site than they think they are going to use in case there are problems. This is the contractor's method of assuring that construction will not be stopped while someone runs out to get more lumber. When the job is completed, the remaining materials belong to the contractor, not the homeowner.

A statement that work will be performed to the specifications listed in *RESIDENTIAL CONSTRUCTION PERFORMANCE GUIDELINES for Professional Builders & Remodelers – 2nd Edition.*

This book is the National Association of Home Builder's bible for what is and is not acceptable. If you and the builder both agree that the job will be built to this standard, you will have little to argue about.

Before you sign the contract and everything is rosy, get the name and cell phone number of the salesman, the contractor, the person who holds the builder's license (it may not be the same person), the construction superintendent and the lead carpenter on your job.

It is amazing. Before the contract is signed everything is wonderful. When something goes wrong, everyone may disappear. If you have their cell phone numbers, you can usually track someone down and get action started.

8   Take the guesswork out of disagreements

Things happen when you build or remodel a house. You picture one thing, the builder-installed reality looks like something else. Quite often this causes high blood pressure, sleepless nights and poor job performance because your real work doesn't get done if you are spending many unproductive hours chasing down the builder, project manager or lead carpenter.

When you finally track down the builder, he often gives little or no satisfaction because he shrugs his shoulders and says "that's the way these things go" or he whips out a change of order form and says that he can fix it but it will cost you extra and will slow down the job so we have to change the completion date.

It is even worse when you have a builder call back. The concrete slab in the garage may have cracked or the vinyl flooring may have lost its adhesion. The bathtub or shower may leak, the new kitchen cabinets may not line up with each other, or the chimney may be separating from the house.

None of these things should have happened. You are paying or have already paid good money and you want the builder to come and make it right.

What does the law say? What does the builder have to do?

If you wrote in the contract that the work would be performed to the specifications listed in *RESIDENTIAL CONSTRUCTION PERFORMANCE GUIDELINES for Professional Builders & Remodelers – 2nd Edition,* you and the builder know what is required.

The book was produced by the NAHB Remodelors Council and The Single Family Small Volume Builders Committee. You can get copies from the NAHB bookstore, (800) 223-2665, or on the Web at www.builderbooks.com.

When something goes wrong on your job, it is not your opinion or what you would like to happen or what the builder wants or has time to do that is required. It is what should be done based upon many years of case law and arbitration. The recommended solutions for 100 common problems are outlined in the book.

Be prepared for the fact that decisions are not always decided in favor of the homeowner. Also the builder is usually only required to repair the problem. You might want him to tear out and re-do the work so that it looks like the idealized picture you saw in a magazine.

You also may inspect the job with a magnifying glass, but the builder may only be required to make it so that it looks good from 20 feet away. There is a good possibility that you may not like the answers in *RESIDENTIAL CONSTRUCTION PERFORMANCE GUIDELINES* but at least you will know what the accepted guidelines are.

If you and the builder do not agree in advance to follow these guidelines, if something happens, you will be stuck with performance based on the builder's good will or the results of an expensive court fight. Even if you might get a better judgment in court, litigation is terribly expensive and there is no guaranty that the builder will have the financial where-with-all to make financial restitution required by the judgment.

If that happens you are stuck with thousands of dollars of court costs and having to get the job re-done at your expense.

OK, so what would the *RESIDENTIAL CONSTRUCTION PERFORMANCE GUIDELINES* have told the builder to do in the cases I outlined?

Cracked concrete slab in the garage
According to the *PERFORMANCE GUIDELINES* "Cracks in concrete garage floor greater than 3/16–inch in width or 1/8-inch in vertical displacement are excessive."

The contractor would have to repair the concrete to meet the guideline by "thoroughly cleaning, filling and troweling the surface using latex-fortified cement mixture or other materials designed to fill cracks and bond concrete."

Vinyl flooring losing its adhesion
PERFORMANCE GUIDELINES states that "Resilient flooring shall not lift, bubble, or detach." The contractor has the option of either repairing or replacing the vinyl. If the pattern has been discontinued or the color is not the same, it is not the contractor's problem.

The bathtub or shower leaks
PERFORMANCE GUIDELINES agrees with you. "Bathtubs and showers shall not leak." The contractor is required to repair the bathtub or shower leak by sealing areas around tubs and showers. Once fixed however, maintenance of caulk seals is the owner's responsibility.

The new kitchen cabinets may not line up with each other
PERFORMANCE GUIDELINES states the cabinet faces "more than 1/8-inch out of line, and cabinet corners more than 3/16–inch out of line, are unacceptable, unless the owner and the contractor agree to disregard the guideline in order to match or otherwise compensate for preexisting conditions."

The corrective measure would be for the contractor to make any adjustment necessary to come within specifications.

Be careful what you ask for. Most existing walls are not straight or plumb. If you complain that the cabinets are not straight, the builder can have them put in a perfectly straight line and, depending upon the preexisting condition of the walls and floors, the result could look far worse than the original condition.

The poor builder may have originally put the cabinets in the way he did to compensate for the condition of your floors and walls. By being too demanding you may have forced the builder to destroy the aesthetic look of your job.

The chimney is separating from the house

PERFORMANCE GUIDELINES states, "newly built fireplaces will often incur slight amounts of separation. The rate of separation from the main structure shall not exceed 1/2-inch in any 10-foot vertical measurement.

The recommended fix by the contractor is to repair the gaps by caulking unless the separation "is due to a structural failure of the chimney foundation itself." If it is a structural problem with the foundation, caulking is not a viable solution and the builder has to repair the problem.

There you have it, five common problems and five solutions. As an individual homeowner who wants the job to be perfect, you may not have been pleased with all of these solutions.

All I can say is that we live in an imperfect world. The solutions outlined in *RESIDENTIAL CONSTRUCTION PERFORMANCE GUIDELINES for Professional Builders & Remodelers – 2nd Edition,* are real world solutions based on the results of hundreds, sometimes thousands of cases of arbitration.

They are fair solutions to which both you and your builder or contractor should be able to agree. If you both agree to abide what is fair upfront, you will both be able to brag about the job when the work is done.

9 You don't own the plans unless you pay for them

If you buy the plans to your modernization up front, or if you go to an architect and have them design the plans and bill you as a separate project, the plans are yours. If you have a design/build contractor design the plans and include the plans in the overall cost of the modernization, the plans belong to him until the job is completed.

Some people thoughtlessly borrow a copy of the plans for their project and get other contractors to bid on the job. That is theft plain and simple. If you want several builders to bid on an identical plan for a room addition, dormer or kitchen remodel, you have to buy the plans up front and then put the job up for bid.

10 How much to pay and when

There are two sets of rules: one for traditional handymen and one for remodeling contractors. The traditional handyman or woman runs a mom and pop operation. He or she may very well run the

business out of a pickup truck. That's not bad. That's good. You do not need a guy packing a lot of overhead to patch a screen door.

A handyman may well need to be paid up front for materials. That's OK, but it is even a better idea if you go with him to the hardware store or lumberyard and pay for the materials yourself. That way you know how much they really cost and your property can't be levied later because the handyman forgot to pay the bill.

In some parts of the country where there are a lot of foreign laborers, foreign-born handymen congregate along street corners or at some home center parking lots. When you hire these gentlemen, and some are very skilled, you are hiring them as day laborers and take on all the responsibilities of a general contractor. You pay them the agreed upon daily wage. You pay for all materials. You pay for the insurance and get the permits or there are none.

Don't take these responsibilities lightly. If you don't get the correct permits and inspections, you can literally see your house go up in smoke. If you don't have the correct homeowners and workmen's compensation insurance coverage, you are electing to self-insure. If Guiermo falls off the roof, you can wind up paying for that accident for the rest of your life. You may also lose your house over it.

Now, let's get to dealing with traditional remodeling contractors.

Some jobs, like roofing and insulation, are quite often done in a day or two. Many good contractors doing this kind of work do not ask for anything until the job is completed.

On larger jobs the procedure is usually to make a small down payment, then pay for the rest of the job in stages as the work is completed.

Ten percent down is usually adequate. Ten percent is enough to cover all the contractor's up-front costs. If a contractor asks for 30% to 50% in advance, be very leery. There is a good chance that he just wants the deposit and may never get around to doing the work.

It may also mean that the contractor is so desperate for money that he may not be in business long enough to complete your job or that he needs your money to complete

work on other people's jobs that he either underbid or has to re-build because of poor workmanship. If any of these things are true, you do not want that contractor to work for you.

The ideal situation is to pay for the job in stages as the proportionate amount of work has been accomplished. The contractor should give you a schedule ahead of time that includes a breakdown of the anticipated costs.

In Michigan and many other states, sub contractors have the right to lien your property if they are not paid. If you have already paid the contractor for their work and their sub contractors have not been paid, you could wind up having to pay for the same work twice. To make certain that this does not happen, do not give the contractor payment for work until he presents you with "Release of Lien" forms signed by the sub contractors who have completed their work, and the suppliers that have supplied the materials for that amount of the job.

In other words if you are supposed to pay 10% upon completion of the concrete and 10% (it may be a greater or smaller amount) upon completion of the rough carpentry, you would want the following:

√ Before making concrete payment, you would want to receive Release of Lien Forms from the concrete subcontractor and the concrete supply company.

√ Before making the rough construction payment, you would want to receive Release of Lien Forms from the Rough Carpentry, Roofing Crews, the Lumber Yard and Roofing Supply Company that supplied the lumber and the roofing supplies.

√ Make certain that the contractor is not paid in full until all work is completed to your satisfaction. Ideally the final payment should equal at least 10% of the entire cost of the job. The more you hold back the faster corrections will be accomplished and the happier you will be with the job. I guarantee it.

11   Why you really need the contractor to pull the permit

Some people think they can save a little time and money and cheat on their property taxes by not applying for the necessary permits. Wrong. The necessary permits entitle you to inspections of the workmanship by skilled inspectors.

I know a good deal more about building and home improvement, but I am not an expert in electrical, plumbing, general construction and heating, ventilation and air conditioning. I doubt if you are either. Pulling the necessary permits and getting the required inspections are our best assurance that the work is up to code.

Besides, if you are caught doing home modernization without pulling the necessary permits, the building inspector has the right to require you to tear everything out, apply for a permit and start from scratch. That can put you a lot of time and many dollars behind the 8-ball.

If you don't get caught during construction, you are still not home free. When it comes time to sell your house, it will, in all probability, be inspected by the local building inspectors. If there are any modifications to your existing house that were made without the proper permits and inspections and are not in their plans, the building inspector has the right to make you tear out the modifications and redo the work getting the proper permits and inspections every step of the way. This can hold up or cause you to lose the sale. It can also take a great deal of your profit margin.

It is also very important for your security that the contractor or the designated trade professional, not you, apply for and pay for all necessary permits. If the contractor applies for and pays for the permits, the building inspector will hold him responsible for the job being built to code. If you apply for the permit, the inspector will hold you responsible. If the job is built wrong, you, not the contractor, will be required to make the necessary changes at your cost.

If the contractor does not want to apply for and pay the permits, it is that he is either not financially solvent or not qualified to pull the permits. There could easily be something wrong with his building license. Whatever the problem is, you do not want that guy anywhere near your job. His price might be right, but you can be pretty certain that his workmanship would not be.

12   How to get something fixed if you think it was done wrong

I have seen more things go wrong on jobs than you can imagine. I have seen roofs put on wrong. Windows put in wrong. Flooring put down on the wrong floors. Anything that you tell me was done wrong on your job I will believe.

Contractors and their sales representatives are wonderful, smiley folk who will do anything to please you. Unfortunately this can change when you tell them something major has gone wrong and they see their profit disappear if they give you the bend over service you have been led to expect.

Give the devil their due. You may have told them one thing and they heard another. You may also have changed your plans mid stream when there was no way they could comply with your new desires. You may also have seen the carpenter or tradesman doing whatever they were doing wrong and not said anything so they thought they were doing it right.

When it comes to a home modernization job, you have to put everything in writing. More than that, you need to take pictures and, if possible, videos to back up your story. If you want a change, get the construction superintendent, lead carpenter or tradesman to make up a formal change order that is dated and signed. Safeguard your copy. It may have to be used in court later.

If you see something going wrong, tell the worker immediately. Call who ever is in charge on the site. Call the construction superintendent for the job and the general contractor/owner of the company.

If the contractor agrees, he will take action to make certain that things are set right. If he does not, you have everything you need to start action or withhold the final payment.

Unfortunately, you may be at fault. Your expectation of perfection may not hold up to a reality check. Reality is not always like the beautiful hand-fired tiles you saw in the photograph, the brilliant hardwood floor in the ad or the magnificent hand blocked wallpaper.

All these items and many more can have naturally occurring imperfections. It's not the contractor's fault. It comes with the territory. The variations add to the value but they can make a perfectionist homeowner hyperventilate.

Even when the imperfection can be traced to a workman's error, the work may be up to accepted methods and practices. Your best defense is to buy a copy of the book, *RESIDENTIAL CONSTRUCTION PERFORMANCE GUIDELINES for Professional Builders & Remodelers – 2nd Edition* that we described earlier. Find out what is and what is not acceptable.

If you add the provision that the work has to be in accordance with the standards set forth in *RESIDENTIAL CONSTRUCTION PERFORMANCE GUIDELINES,* the contractor has to comply to those standards. If not, he has to have the job done over. However, you have to understand that this is a two edged sword. If the job has been done up to accepted job specifications, the job stands, even if it is not up to your desires.

If the builder does not want the "Standards" included in the contract, find another builder fast.

13 What to do if the job is not done on time

First off, if you put a penalty clause giving money off the contract every day the job is late, you can at least get money to assuage your pain. But for most of us that is a hollow victory. The first thing you have to determine is whether the job is really late or you are being impatient.

Go back to Tip # 5 and see how your job compares to the norm. If your job is out of line with the maximum time frame, try to find out why. Did you change plans mid stream? Are cabinets or other items out of stock and unable to be delivered so the builder could not complete the job even with the best will in the world?

Have you contacted the contractor, construction supervisor and the lead carpenters and tried to find out why the job is not being completed? I always tell people to get the cell phone numbers and home phone numbers of the important people on the job. They may not return the calls to the office but they usually answer their cell phone.

If the contractor has just stopped work on your job for no good reason, send him or her a 15-day completion letter. This is a certified letter that tells the contractor that if the work is not completed in 15 business days, you will turn the job over to your attorney and will file complaints with the Building Inspector, the State Building Department and possibly the State Police.

If that does not get some action out of the contractor, nothing will. It is time to consider litigation. Sadly, family attorneys seldom have much knowledge of Builder Law. If your State has a detailed body of law regarding residential construction, shop for a specialist in that field.

14   How to fire a contractor

Very carefully. It is very hard to fire a contractor once work has begun. Even if you throw him off the job with the work half done, or even if he stops work for several months, leaving you hanging, he may still have the legal right to be paid the full contract price of the job even though another contractor has completed the work.

If you have to fire a contractor it is best to have it done by your attorney. Make certain that your attorney has actually checked your state's building laws to see what rights you have.

15 How to shop for a used house

The old saw is that when shopping for a house, the three most important things are location, location, location. That is very true but, once you buy the house, it does not matter how convenient it is to everything, you are still going to have to live in it. Here are some shopping tips.

There are many advantages to buying a used home. The landscaping is in. You know what the neighborhood will look like. The basics have all been paid for. They can even be a bargain, unlike cars which depreciate in value drastically. Homes usually appreciate in value as long as they are in good condition. Sometimes the land under a used house is more valuable than the house itself. Many people will pay $200,000 to $400,000 for a house in a very desirable area only to tear it down and build a more expensive home on the premises.

There are many types of used houses: "first homes", "fixer-uppers", rentals, mid-range homes, "almost new homes" and luxury homes. You should look at each a little differently.

First homes are usually smaller and more affordable but you often grow out of them fast. **Fixer-uppers** are bargains but need a lot of work. You have to have the necessary skills and enjoy putting sweat equity into your living space. They can save you a lot of money or be a very costly mistake.

Rentals are often bargain real estate. They have to be in good enough condition to let the landlord rent out the unit and make enough to pay taxes, mortgage payments, repairs and a small profit. If you aren't cut out to be a landlord or keep up the necessary repairs, they can start costing you money big time.

Location is also very important. A house is not a bargain that is going to make you a lot of money if it is not in a location where people want to live. There are some very successful people who make a great deal of money being what are sometimes called "slum land lords." This advice is not for them. If you are someone like me, John or Jean average, do not buy rental property located in a part of town you would not feel safe going to collect the rent late at night.

A good landlord should never be obtrusive, however, he or she has to know what is going on all the time. Make certain any rental property you buy is close enough to your house for you to keep an eye on things. I promise you, you will be rushing over there to solve a problem in the middle of the night. As a general rule, things break down at all the wrong times and tenants do not give a darn about your schedule. Make sure the property is convenient to you.

Mid range homes are for the second time homebuyer who want more room but don't want the hassle of buying new.

Almost new homes are my favorites. They are just a few years old so they have most of the latest amenities, are completely decorated and fully landscaped and, best of all, enough time as elapsed so that all the dealer callbacks have already been made. The flip side of this is that they can also be lemons the original owners bailed out on because they couldn't handle the problems.

Luxury homes have everything: size, location, and designer-quality accouterments. They usually also have the price tag that goes with these elements. If price tag is easy on the eyes you either got very lucky or should be very suspicious.

No matter what type of used home you are looking at, the first thing you need is a good home inspection. Not all home inspectors are created equal so make certain that the person you hire comes well recommended and is accredited by one of the national associations.

Know what the charges are going to be before you give the go-ahead. I remember one case where the homeowner thought the inspection report was going to cost a couple of hundred bucks and the final bill was over $10,000. The bill wound up in court. You do not need that type of aggravation.

You still have the responsibility. The home inspector is not expected to be an expert at heating and cooling equipment, electrical, waterproofing, insulation or structural engineering. If the furnace goes out 10 minutes after you move in, it's not the inspector's fault. He is just a generalist. He will check on a few things, but there are hundreds of things that can go wrong that he will not, and is not required to know anything about.

In other words, you are the buyer. You are paying the inspector X amount of money to look at the house, but you can't shift your responsibility to him. This does not mean you shouldn't get a home inspector. It just means that you should not invest him with super human powers.

Call an expert. If you or the inspector are suspicious about anything, get the opinion of a specialist right away. But be sure to find out the cost of the expert's inspection before you give the go-ahead. A few hundred dollars is OK. A cost of several thousand for the inspection might make you want to reconsider the house.

Special things you should look out for in older homes are the structural integrity and condition of the roof and basement. The top and bottom of the house.

Make certain that you or someone you trust goes up on the roof and inspects the shingles, vents, valleys and gutters carefully. Also go into the attic and check the underside of the roof and the quantity, thickness and condition of the insulation. Rigid, matted fiberglass insulation can be a sign of past water damage. Pick up some of the insulation to make certain that the decking under it is in good condition.

This is also a good time to determine whether there are adequate soffit and attic vents. Most older homes do not have sufficient insulation or ventilation. Many homes that are 40 or 50 years old do not have any insulation in the walls. Many have gable vents that do more harm than good. Most will not have sufficient soffit and ridge or roof vents. These are upgrades that you should plan on making the first year.

Go down to the basement and check the walls for cracks, sloping or signs of water damage. Check the basement floor for heaving. Sniff for a mold sent. If you can smell the scent of mold, it is there, somewhere. Don't be satisfied until you know where. Mold could be a serious problem. In extreme cases it could cause you to lose or have to move out of the house. Make certain that a problem exists before it becomes your problem. If you have the least doubt, either don't buy or have a physical test done to make certain that you do not have a problem.

While you are sniffing, sniff for cat and dog urine smells. Pets are wonderful but their presence often lingers on long after they have gone. If you smell pet odors in the basement or on the main floors, you are going to have to do a great deal of work. I'll get into how to get rid of pet and smoke odors in my upcoming painting and sealing book.

If you love the house, it may not be a deal breaker, BUT it is going to require weeks of work and you will not be able to stand living in the place until that work is done. Put all this into your buying equation.

Now, look up and check the water pipes. Are the water supply lines copper or iron? Iron pipes will have to be replaced.

How about the electrical? Do you have a fuse box or a circuit breaker panel? How much power does the house have? It is not uncommon for older homes to have 60-amp service. If you are into a lot of electrical sound or computer equipment, you probably will eventually upgrade to 200-amp service. 150-amps is the minimum needed for a modern house. If you do not have sufficient amps, you have to upgrade.

Check the heating and air-conditioning systems and the water heater for age and operating condition. Is the water heater big enough to provide sufficient hot water for your family? If there is just one or two of you, an old 40-gallon water heater may be fine for a while. But if there are 4 or 5 in the family upgrading will be a requirement.

On the main floors check the walls and ceilings for signs of leakage or patching. Water leaks are a good possibility in bathrooms and kitch-ens. Look for them. Carefully sniff for mold. Here again, if you find anything suspicious, call for an air quality inspection. This may be at your cost, but if you are interested in the house, it is worth it.

Are windows single or double pane? If single, you will probably wind up buying new windows. Do the windows open and close easily? How about the doors? Are they and the locks in good condition?

How about the floors? Do you love them or hate them? Can you live with them or have to replace them?

Are the bedrooms big enough? Many older homes do not have enough storage space.

Now to the most important rooms in the house, the kitchen and bath(s). I call them the heart and lungs of the home. Many women look at almost new kitchens and decide to tear out everything. That's OK. They are entitled. But understand that you can easily drop $25,000 to $50,000 in a kitchen.

If the kitchen is too small for your needs, there is no way to expand it without moving walls or adding on to the house. If you do not have the money to upgrade the kitchen and you can't live with the kitchen as it exists, you will not be happy in the house.

I will now add a thoroughly sexist bit of advice to any husbands reading this book. It does not matter if your wife is the CEO of an automobile company or Governor of a State and does not have the time to even walk into the kitchen.

If that kitchen is not up to her standards and the family budget does not allow you to make it that way, you are not going to be a happy camper. If your wife is not happy with the kitchen, it does not matter that everything else is wonderful and the seller just wants pennies on the dollar. Take my advice and look for another house.

The bath(s) are almost as important. On a square foot basis they are the most expensive area in the house. If you can't live with the master bath and do not have a great sense of humor, you may want to look for another house.

16 How to shop for a new house

Just because a home is new does not mean that it is trouble free. If you are buying a spec home, hire a home inspector to check it out.

When buying from a builder's model, find out how the electrical and insulation compares to BOCA code. Find out how much it will cost you to get the home upgraded to BOCA code.

If you like the house, ask for a list of builders options. Many of those options, like better flooring, adding extra insulation or special lighting are best done while the home is being constructed. Building a deck or putting in pavers can be done anytime and you will usually save money by not having them done by the builder.

You have to understand many builders price their homes to be competitive and make their money on so-called options.

Buying a new home is a very emotional time of your life. It is a thoroughly thrilling experience. You will save yourself a lot of heartbreak if you understand a couple of things going into the experience.

Most homes are not completed when they are promised. Most homes are more expensive than you believe they will be going into the transaction. If your home is even half as desirable as you think it is, you will never have the upper hand.

Get rough with him and the builder may give you back your deposit, add about ten or twenty grand to the price of the house and sell it to the next family waiting in line. This may be a moral victory, but you will not have the house.

This being the case, the location of the house, the beauty of the subdivision, the perfection of the plan mean next to nothing. The reputation of the builder, his honesty, integrity and sense of fair dealing mean everything.

If you do the work needed to find a great builder, if you search out and check references, you will have a happy experience. If you rush into something and leave the checking up to dumb luck, you are being dumb and will be out of luck.

17 Where to find a great homebuilder

A great builder is a man or woman who builds houses filled with happy people. If the building experience was a good one, the homebuyers will brag about him. I say him because many builders are men, but more and more of the most successful builders are women or man/woman building teams.

There is a difference in the sexes. Women are often more perceptive to your wants and have better communication skills. Those can be big assets for a builder.

It just makes sense that if you are interviewing builders to build your house, you would want to talk to buyers who came before you. When asked about their builder, happy homebuyers will tell you how he or she worked with them and listened to them. He met deadlines and kept the buyers informed at all times. If things were done wrong, he admitted it and corrected the problem promptly.

After the buyers moved into their new home and found problems, he responded immediately and sent crews promptly to correct whatever was wrong.

If you are using an architect, he will tell you the names of builders he or she works with frequently. That's a great benefit but doesn't let you off the hook. You will be living in the house long after the architect has forgotten your name. Make certain the builder is someone you feel comfortable with and has lots of happy homeowners.

You can bet your bottom dollar that the builder is going to check out your finances and credit worthiness. Return the compliment. Have your bank check his finances and give you the assurance that he is up to the job.

By the way, this is not just something you should do with a small custom builder. In many ways it is even easier for that big builder constructing hundreds of houses in several subdivisions to have cash flow and credit problems.

These problems can lead to production delays, shoddy workmanship, maybe bankruptcy. You could lose everything or it might take years for you to gain clear title. You don't want to become a statistic so make certain that your builder is worthy of you.

18   What the Building Code means

When a home is constructed, it must be built to meet certain minimum standards in order for the local building inspector to issue a "Certificate of Occupancy." Technically these standards are set by each of the fifty sovereign states and modified by local jurisdictions.

There are also three national and international bodies that create their own model codes. There are the Council of American Building Officials (CABO), the Building Officials and Code Officials (BOCA), the International conference of Building Officials (ICBO) and the Southern Building Code Congress International (SBCCI).

In 2003, three of these organizations, the BOCA, ICBO and SBCCI groups, merged to create the International Code Council (ICC). The new ICC Building Code will cover the entire country.

Most states adopt and may slightly modify one of the national codes. Michigan presently has a less stringent code but is considering upgrading its code to conform to the higher standards of the rest of the nation.

In addition, a county or a local governmental body can require that the state code be surpassed. In other words the city or county can say our homes have to be built better than the state code. They cannot say that homes can be built to a lesser standard.

In addition to the building codes, the governing bodies of the Electrical, Plumbing, and Heating Ventilation and Air conditioning (HVAC) associations create their own codes for their specialties. State Governments adopt these codes.

When a new home is built, it has to be built to the prevailing standards of the various building, electrical, plumbing and HVAC codes as designated by the State, County or Municipal governments. Each area of specialization has their own inspectors who work in cooperation with each other to check to see that the work in their various specialties is "up to code".

The building inspector inspects the house at critical times during the construction process. Since much of the electrical, plumbing and HVAC work must be done before the drywall is up. The inspectors for these specialties must inspect the basic work before the walls are covered. After the walls are up, the final work by electricians, plumbers and HVAC contractors is performed and final inspections are made.

19 Why Code Plus Construction is worth it

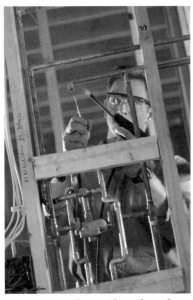

Code Plus means that you are getting the "good" stuff. Above code insulation, heating, cooling, electrical, plumbing, floors, windows and roofing. Most new homes in America are "built to code". "Built to code" means that the house meets the minimum acceptable standards necessary for the building and specialty inspectors to certify the house as being inhabitable.

In a state like Michigan that has a less stringent building code, this may mean that the house does not even meet the national codes. Calling for Code Plus construction in such cases may merely mean that the house is good enough to meet the national code.

Code Plus often means using innovative building materials and techniques like Structural Insulated Panels (SIPs) and Insulated Concrete Forms (ICFs). Structural insulated panels (SIPs) are made of a rigid layer of polyurethane or polystyrene insulating foam sandwiched between layers of 7/16-inch oriented-strand board (OSB). Insulated Concrete Forms are foam block and concrete. Both types of materials can be used to build better-insulated, stronger, tighter, more mold resistant homes.

In most cases "code plus" means that someone took the time to specify quality features above those required by the building, electrical, plumbing and heating, ventilation and air conditioning (HVAC) codes.

In addition, the NAHB Building America program tests, then recommends various upgrades. You'll find specifics on Code Plus options in almost every section of this book.

20 Why you want an ENERGY STAR home

An ENERGY STAR® Labeled Home

Address

Built by

Verified by

Date

Optional Information

This home has been individually verified by an independent professional to meet ENERGY STAR guidelines for energy efficiency. ENERGY STAR labeled homes protect the environment by using less energy.
www.energystar.gov

By now we are used to seeing ENERGY STAR labels on appliances, windows, furnaces and air conditioners. But did you know that you can buy an entire house with an ENERGY STAR label?

Believe it or not you can buy an entire house with an ENERGY STAR label. When you see the label, you know that the builder is taking the effort to give you a much better house.

ENERGY STAR is a federal program sponsored by the Department of Energy. You can find out all the details on the program's web site, www.energystar.gov.

ENERGY STAR is often offered as a special kind of Code Plus option. A builder may offer to upgrade the house to meet ENERGY STAR standards. These upgrades usually do so much to decrease heating and cooling bills that they pay for themselves in just a few years, but you continue to save for as long as you own the house.

If I were new house hunting, the first thing I would ask the builder or his salesman would be if they built ENERGY STAR houses or offered an ENERGY STAR upgrade.

A builder can't just tell you that his houses are ENERGY STAR. An independent testing company tests each house individually. If the house achieves the necessary points, it gets the label. A house gets more points for having a 96 percent energy efficient furnace than a 90 percent efficient furnace. It gets more points for having R-49 attic insulation than R-30.

The average house has thousands of small holes in the building

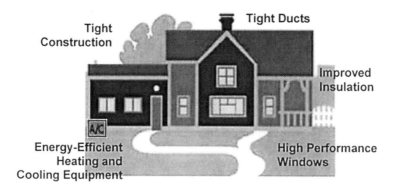

envelope. An ENERGY STAR home has a tightly sealed building envelope that has been tested for air leakage.

According to the Department of Energy, tight ducts are very important because the ductwork in the average house is so leaky that 20 to 30 percent of the heated or cooled air leaks out before it can get to its destination. ENERGY STAR homes are tested to make certain the ductwork has few leaks.

Many new homes are poorly insulated with gaps in some areas and over-packing in others. Often soffit ventilation channels are covered because insulation has been installed in a haphazard manner. Insulation in an ENERGY STAR home is inspected to insure that it has been installed without gaps, crimping or compression so that it insulates and seals.

An ENERGY STAR house has high performance windows that carry the ENERGY STAR label. In Michigan that means that the windows have a U-factor of 0.35 or less.

An ENERGY STAR house must have at least a 90 percent efficient furnace and air conditioning must be properly sized and rated at 12 SEER or higher.

Every builder claims to build a superior home but ENERGY STAR homes have been tested by an independent third party, so perspective buyers know they are getting the added quality and value for which they are paying. Homebuyers receive a certificate showing that the home is within ENERGY STAR guidelines.

If you are new home shopping, I have no doubt that you will be more comfortable and save on energy costs by buying an ENERGY STAR home. It is usually the best value that you can get for your money.

21 Builder upgrades vs doing it yourself later

New car dealers cannot advertise a base model car price unless they have at least one for sale on the lot. If they do not have the car for sale, they can be charged with bait and switch advertising.

New home builders do it all the time. Builders advertise base prices for their houses but seldom, if ever, build a house to the basic specifications. Instead they load the model up with one or two fireplaces, deluxe cabinetry, granite counter tops, hardwood flooring, better appliances, a jetted tub, pavers, an exotic wood deck, hardwood door and side lights, chandelier and a two story entrance way.

Naturally you fall in love with everything you see and you may not find out that these are all extra cost options until the salesman starts totaling up the final cost of the house. Upgrades are often drastically over priced. It is common for a builder to increase the true cost of the upgrade by 50% to 100% or more. Often all they have to do is make a phone call and someone else does all the work.

You owe it to yourself to price out some of the goodies and see if you could save a bundle by having them installed after you buy. For instance you could easily buy the deck, pavers, appliances and chandelier after closing day. A beautiful mural in the children's room can also be painted after the fact and you can usually negotiate a credit for the appliances and then go out and buy the appliances you prefer. Some builders will give you a credit and send you off to the local distributors showroom.

Things I would always suggest that you have installed during construction include: windows, sprayed-in insulation, sound conditioning, furnace, air conditioning and hot water heater upgrades.

The rule of thumb is to determine what you could buy the upgrade for yourself on the open market and then find out what the builder wants to charge you for an upgrade. If the cost for the upgrade is less than 3-times what it would cost to do later, do it at the time of construction.

Chapter II
Major Projects

22 Do your homework before doing the deed

The best way to make certain that your home improvement is what you want it to be is to know what you want before going to an architect or modernization contractor. I don't mean that you should know the exact size, or floor plan or be able to specify the lighting fixtures; but that you should have decided upon the extra needs you want to meet and the feel of the final construction.

Don't play "Twenty Questions" with the builder
Unless you know what you want, the designer or builder have to play "Twenty Questions" with you or guess what you want. Both of these methods usually miss the mark and leave homeowners steaming.

Some of the things you may be looking for are: more room for entertaining, storage, better lighting, and a truly luxurious shower. The feel of the final construction may be: modern, homey, "like it was part of the original construction," rich.

People who don't do their homework before going to a designer or builder usually get "inspired" and start making changes after the final plans have been made and construction started. This not only slows down construction it adds expense big time.

Make a file
To make certain this does not happen to you dedicate a file box and a notebook to the project. Six months to a year before you plan to start the job, start going to home shows, touring builders model homes, and reading home and design magazines and catalogues with special care. Go window shopping at places like Home Expo Design Center and specialty flooring, electrical and plumbing supply stores. If you are planning a kitchen or bath, go to all the kitchen and bath stores in the neighborhood.

Whenever you see something you like, try to get literature or a picture of it. Make notes and explore the topics on the Internet. Copies of everything you find should go into your file box. Pretty soon you will have to start special files for flooring, fixtures, windows, etc. It is important that you also start getting a handle on pricing so that you can get a realistic idea of the affordability of your dreams.

Make notes of needs: sound conditioning in the walls so the kids can entertain their friends without disturbing the rest of the family, big picture windows over-looking the garden, one of the new bubble tubs, hydronic radiant floor heating.

Organize
A couple weeks before contacting a builder or architect organize your thoughts and have heart to heart meetings with your significant other and the rest of the family. Everyone be on the same page and know what you are trying to achieve before going to the professionals.

Togetherness pays
If you have a husband, wife or significant other, it is important that you meet with the professionals together. That way both of you get input and both of you have the opportunity to shoot down a bad idea before it takes on a life of its own.

Don't get sucker punched by letting your dearly beloved say he or she is too busy and has full confidence in your judgment. As flattering as that sounds, in your heart of hearts you know that if something goes wrong and your heart's delight thinks your decision a bad one, that negative feeling can fester for years.

Even with a super intelligent soul mate such as yours, it is very easy for a man to think that a solution offered by a builder is a great idea and for the woman he loves to think that idea is just plain awful (or the other way around).

Put it in writing

Give your ideas to the architect, designer or builder in writing. Show them some of your clippings (they may want to keep some). At the same time, let them know that these are just thought starters, not ironclad demands. A good professional will see many ways of enhancing your ideas and making the unaffordable, affordable. You are paying them a handsome fee to make your dreams come true. Give them the flexibility to do the job.

23 Include Universal Design for a great life

If you were 38 in 2003, you will be 65 by 2030. You won't be alone. It is estimated that 20 percent of the population will be 65 or older. Eighty-five percent of the older population wants to stay in their homes for as long as they live.

If you plan to stay in your present house and would like to remain for the rest of your life, it just makes sense to make it as user friendly as possible. I know that many of you will think that this information is just for the other guy because your house is fine.

It doesn't really work that way. If you have a belly button, you are getting older. It doesn't really matter if you work out at the health club every day, your body is getting older. Even a young person in excellent physical condition can break a leg skiing or fall off a ladder while doing a simple chore.

Your house has to grow to meet your future needs

Many of the things about your house that are perfectly fine for a healthy thirty-something are open invitations to the emergency ward when you are over 65.

Take lighting as an example. Most of our houses have barely adequate lighting. You didn't notice when you moved in and have adjusted to it over the years. Making those adjustments become harder and harder every year over 50.

Light up your life

By the time a person reaches 60 only one-third the amount of light reaches the retina as that perceived by a 20-year old. That means that the world is darker and much harder to see. Especially inside a house where we are forced to rely on artificial light. A major cause of home accidents among the over 65 crowd is that they bump into, trip over or fall off of things they can't see. Improve lighting now and you may save yourself needless trips to the hospital later.

I'm not talking about buying a couple lamps and plugging them into already over-loaded circuits. Unless you have recently upgraded your lighting, your home probably needs recessed lighting and/or large fluorescent fixtures in every major room of the house. Add improved hall and entrance lighting, as well as spotlights, task and under cabinets lighting, maybe even skylights, in the kitchen and bath. The goal should be to eliminate shadows and have plentiful, even light throughout the house.

Make rooms a joy to use

Some upgrades that you should seriously consider are enlarging the kitchen and master bath and adding a first floor master bedroom and laundry room if you do not already have them.

If you have a colonial, I know that you probably have a beautiful master bedroom upstairs. If your house has a basement and is over 20-years-old, the washing machine and dryer are probably in the basement.

These features can be fine in your 20's and 30's, but add 20 or 30 years, thirty extra pounds, bifocals and a dose of arthritis in the knees and hips and those journeys up and down the stairs are pain-filled accident magnets.

Spoil yourself happy

Many of the changes that you should make to your kitchen and bathroom are things that you would love to have and may have been denying yourself for years. "Spoiling" yourself with extra room and luxury features now when you can afford it or have the earning power to pay for it, is a practical way to make your home more livable in the future.

In the bath some of the "indulgent necessities" include large, 0-clearance showers with benches, grab bars and hand held showerheads, comfort height toilets and pedestal lavatories. In the kitchen they include lowered stovetops, multi-height countertops and sit-down work areas.

If we include the principles of Universal Design into our home modifications now, we can do so beautifully. If we wait until modifications are done on an emergency basis, they may be made by someone who cares little about the aesthetics.

Learn from the best, forget the rest

Reza Ahmadi and Dr. Kay Hodson Carlton, two professors at Ball State University, are Co-project Directors of the WellCome Home Project. With the help of many leaders in their respective fields they have developed an excellent web site, www.bsu.edu/wellcomehome/ that goes into detail on the modifications an older or disabled person may need to live comfortably. Mary Jo Perterson authored the friendly kitchen segment. Ms. Peterson's book, *Universal Kitchen and Bathroom Planning: Design That Adapts to People*, is considered by many to be one of the most authoritative in the field.

The WellCome Home site is filled with "must know" information that should be studied carefully by anyone considering modifying his or her present home or looking for a new one. It also has a great deal of very practical tips for anyone trying to help modify a loved one's house so that they, too, can age in place.

Wheelchair bound people have limited access
From information on the site I learned that a person seated in a wheel chair has a useful vertical range starting at 15-inches from the floor and extending to 48-inches off the floor. The average standing person has a useful range from 24-inches from the floor to 72-inches off the floor. That range shortens as we grow older, muscles weaken and arthritis sets in.

A kitchen working area should have a 5-foot by 5-foot open space to enable a person in a wheel chair to turn around and 32-inch wide doors and passageways.

I asked my executive editor, Kathleen, to take these criteria and apply them to the kitchen of her 50-year old ranch.

Kathleen was crushed. If confined to a wheelchair, her only accessible work area was the kitchen table. The only appliance she could use was the microwave. The only storage she could reach were the upper shelves of three lower cabinets. Her pantry, stove, refrigerator/ freezer, sink and dishwasher, as well as the majority of her lower cabinets and all upper cabinets were inaccessible.

When she took similar measurements in the master bath, the results were just as disheartening. Add to these problems, the fact that both Kathleen and her husband have already had close calls carry-ing laundry baskets up and down the basement stairs. Kathleen and her husband have some serious decisions to make. Clearly they have to improve or move.

Learn the principles of Universal Design and apply them to your house. They are not just for old people or people with physical impairments. They make homes more comfortable, safer and a great deal more user-friendly for every-

24 Remodeling has its own set of rules

Your marriage may depend on your remodeler

Your contractor is far more important to your marriage and has a far greater impact on your sanity and your bank account than your brother-in-law. Pat Murphy, a friend of mine who is considered to be one of the best building inspectors in the business always tells people two things:

"Quite a few remodeling jobs end in divorce. Living through a major remodel is the acid test of a marriage. If you can't live with extreme stress, don't remodel."

"No matter what the builder promises you, expect a mess. Building trades almost never clean up after themselves. Even when they think they have been extremely careful, you may be horrified."

Make certain the production manager knows your needs

Before construction starts meet with the production manager and spell out the ground rules for the job. He may not be able to comply with them but at least you will have a common point of reference.

If there are days that they cannot be at your house, tell him. If you have very valuable but delicate plants that must be protected, tell him. Anything that is important to you should be put in writing. One copy stays with the production manager. The other copy is signed by him or her and put in your job file.

Play fair

Your 16-year old daughter should not be running around in a bra and skimpy-shorts if you expect any work to get done. Movement around the house has to be limited. It is fine to inspect, maybe even photograph, the work while the job is progressing. Just don't get in the way.

Most craftspeople love dogs. They probably have a couple of them at home and may even have one in the truck. That does not mean that your dog belongs on the job site. He may be loved by all but he does not make a good building inspector. No matter how well trained, he will get in the way, could cause an accident and might be hurt or killed. Keep him away from the workmen.

You want the crew to work. Do your best to stay out of their hair and make it as easy for them to do their job as possible.

25 Adding on doesn't add up if it destroys the look

I love to see houses growing up or out. It means that the owners love the house and the neighborhood and are making their home grow to fit their needs.

Technically a room addition is when you add on to the existing level of the house. A dormer is when you add an additional story to your home.

Done well, additions and dormers can add a great deal of value to your home. Done badly, they can destroy the look of a home and make it very hard to sell.

A room addition or a dormer should look like it is a natural out-growth of the house. Contractors who specialize in this type of work like to brag that they can make an addition or dormer look like it was part of the original house.

Additions are the easiest, most natural progression. If it looks like it was added in the back or to the side, that's fine, just as long as it's attractive. I've been to housing seminars in which architects and builders bragged about the sprawling extensions of some of their designs. They were deliberately using different materials to give the home an established look, like it had been added on to over the years.

If a high priced architect brags about how his use of different materials makes the home look like it has grown over the years in his high priced design, I guess it's OK for you to add a family room in the back and use vinyl siding rather than the face brick that covers the rest of the house.

Adding up is tricky. The technique for building dormers was invented by the owners of a Detroit-based building company many years ago. It was such a novel building method that they were able to patent the concept. The company, Fairway Construction, is still building dormers today.

A dormer is an excellent idea when there is not sufficient land to add on. It does, however, take a very high level of skill for a builder to add up than add on.

During construction, the first thing the builder does is tear off the existing roof. Then he very quickly adds a knee wall, adds roof trusses and roof deck boards. No one breathes easy until the dormer is enclosed and the house has regained its structural integrity and is once again protected from the elements.

Done well, a dormer looks like a natural extension of the house. It can turn a nice ranch or bungalow into a beautiful colonial. Designed and built badly it can be an unmitigated disaster.

A critical aspect of dormer design is the placement of the stairs leading from the first to second floor. Room for that stairway was not designed into the house. The builder or architect has to place it so that it looks like a natural progression.

With all these potentials for disaster it is especially important when considering a second story dormer addition that you use only a builder and architect with a good track record on similar designs.

It is very vital that you not only get the names of references and give them a call, but to

26 Kitchens were made for cooking not just looking

The kitchen is not just the heart of the home it is the site of the most expensive remodeling jobs. Every year at the National Association of Home Builders show the country's leading remodeling contractors tell me that the most expensive kitchen remodels are demanded by the people who will use them the least.

One remodeler loves to tell about the client who said expense was no object; she wanted the very best of everything but didn't want to know how to use anything. Her kitchen was just for show.

Not too many years ago a nicely remodeled kitchen cost $25,000. Today that figure can easily reach $125,000. If that is your desire, I am delighted. You are doing your part to keep the economy strong. If you just want a good, workmanlike kitchen, here are a few pointers that may help you.

Donald E. Silvers is a nationally known chef and kitchen designer who lives in California but designs kitchens for people all around the country. Silvers designs for people who really like to cook and want to do so with maximum efficiency. Here are a few of his ideas.

1. Divide your kitchen into two areas. One area for storage and cleaning and a second area for food preparation.

    The storage and cleaning area should be located as close as possible to the door you will bring in food supplies. It should contain your dry storage, dishes and dishwasher. If at all possible, it should also have its own sink. Dirty dish stacking and cleaning are confined to the storage and cleaning area. It also becomes a second food preparation area if you have two cooks working together. This way no one gets in the other person's way while working.

    The food preparation area holds the stove, refrigerator, sink and most food preparation tools. It is the main work-station for cooking. Since it is entirely separate from the cleaning area, the cook never has to work around a sink full of dirty dishes when he wants to clean vegetables or drain pasta.

2. If you add six inches of depth to kitchen counters, you can store all your most used small kitchen appliances in plain site on the kitchen counter. You find them instantly and can use them easily. If you love your food processor, blender, pasta maker and bread machine the way many cooks do, you have to believe that this is a truly awesome idea.

3. Vinyl is the best floor covering as well as the least expensive It is comfortable to stand on, easy to clean and often resilient enough so that falling dishes and glassware seldom break when they fall.

This was just a taste test. If you'd like to learn more, get a copy of Don Silver's book, "Kitchen Design with Cooking in Mind." It is available for $29.95 from Amazon.com or direct from the author at (800) 900-4761, or on his web site at www.donsilvers.com. If you become completely enthralled with the way he thinks, you can call Silvers and he will review your plans or design a kitchen for you for a surprisingly affordable fee.

27   When it comes to cabinets looks can be deceiving

The most important, most expensive, and least understood parts of any kitchen remodel are the cabinets. If you have appliances you don't like, you can replace them without disturbing the rest of the kitchen. The same is true with the fixtures, even the countertops and floors. But if you don't like the cabinets, or they are starting to break down, it means the entire kitchen has to be torn apart.

Every kitchen cabinet in every kitchen display looks good. How to choose cabinets that will hold up well and stay looking good is the $64,000 question. According to Larry Wilson of Merillat, the nation's largest cabinetmaker, about half of all cabinets are made by a local cabinetmaker, which means they do not have the backing of a national company. They may be just as good or even better than those made by the big boys, but there is no way for you to tell, unless you know what to look for.

To get this information my staff and I asked manufacturers, installers and big and small kitchen and bath remodeling companies what to look for in a quality cabinet. Not every good cabinet has all the features listed here, but this list is a good way for you to weigh the pros and cons of different manufacturers' products.

Cabinets are made of four major ingredients: the cabinet itself, which is called "the box" in the trade; the shelves; the door; and the drawer. And then there are the design elements such as the finish, decorative hardware, molding, etc., that add to the cabinets' appeal.

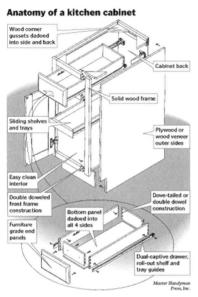

Anatomy of a kitchen cabinet

Wood corner gussets dadoed into side and back

Cabinet back

Solid wood frame

Sliding shelves and trays

Plywood or wood veneer outer sides

Easy clean interior

Double doweled front frame construction

Bottom panel dadoed into all 4 sides

Dove-tailed or double dowel construction

Furniture grade end panels

Dual-captive drawer, roll-out shelf and tray guides

Master Handyman Press, Inc.

Here's what to look for in each area:

The box

Sturdy, square, symmetrical construction of the box is important. There should be nothing fragile about a cabinet. It should be built on a square within very close tolerances. All the same size and style cabinets should be identical. There should be no variations due to sloppy workmanship.

Frame Vs. frameless

Cabinets can be either framed or frameless. The standard American style is framed construction. This means you see a frame on all four sides of the cabinet front, and doors and drawer front panels overlap the frame. Door hinges are attached to the frame.

Frameless construction is a European influence and is found most often in Euro-style cabinetry. In frameless construction, there is no front frame. Since no frame exists, doors and drawers do not overlap. They slide directly into the cabinet. Many people like this more tailored appearance.

As a practical matter, frameless construction is considered to be a little stronger than framed cabinetry. Frameless construction also provides a bit more useable room in the cabinet because no allowance has to be made for the width of the frame when placing dishes.

Solid wood Vs. veneer

There is a lot of discussion as to whether solid wood or veneer-covered engineered wood is best. There is no "best." Which you choose is up to you.

The perception is that solid wood is superior. It has all of wood's beauties, strengths and weaknesses. Solid wood is solid. However, it moves with changes in temperature and humidity. It dries out and becomes smaller, loosening joints. It absorbs humidity and swells slightly. When loose, it can squeak. It becomes brittle and splinters or cracks when dry. Solid wood doors are usually made of several pieces of wood glued together. That means that there can be variations in the finish.

Wood veneer is peeled, not sawed. A veneer surface over engineered wood is therefore more uniform than solid wood. Engineered wood doesn't expand or contract and is engineered for a specific purpose. If the correct engineered wood is used in cabinet construction, it cannot be beat.

Purists prefer real wood. Most practical people are very happy and get better results with veneer-covered engineered wood.

The frame is no place for engineered wood. Inner edges should be profiled or rounded on the inside to eliminate scrapes and splinters. Outside profiles should be sharp 90-degree angles for uniform cabinet-to-cabinet installation.

Look for wood gussets. While every manufacturer uses gussets at the top of their base cabinets, wood gussets dadoed into the sides are strongest. Looking for wood gussets is important because with the new solid, granite and even concrete counter tops, the base cabinets are supporting a tremendous amount of weight. The stronger the gusset, the greater the stability of the cabinet.

The back of the cabinet should be composed of at least 1/8-inch to 1/4-inch plywood dadoed into the base and sides. Walls are not perfectly flat. A good back panel is necessary for the cabinets to hang properly and look uniform. Some makers save money by not putting backs in their cabinets. They figure that you don't see the back, so why bother? The back provides a great deal of the cabinets' structural integrity. It is a good idea to back away from backless cabinets.

Outer sides, which means any exposed side, should be solid wood, plywood, or as is often the case with quality cabinets, veneer-covered plywood. Scuff and wear resistance is very important here, especially for base cabinets.

The interior should be an easy care surface that matches the exterior of the cabinet.

Photo courtesy of KraftMaid

Shelves

Shelving should be a minimum of 1/2-inch thick; 3/4-inch is better. Weak shelving often needs a support in the middle of the back. All your heavy pots and pans, plus heirloom dishes and glassware, will be on these shelves. You don't want them to let go.

Shelving should be adjustable with very sturdy die-cast shelf rests. It should also extend the full depth of the cabinet. Rollout shelves are a blessing. However, some designers believe that every bottom base cabinet shelf should be a roll out. They cost more, but they turn dead space into easy-to-use space. If you're over 40, they really save the back.

Historically plates and mixing bowls, etc. are stored and often displayed in upper cabinets. The older you get, the heavier they get. Some base cabinet designs now store plates and heavy bowls in lower pull out shelving. If it is easier for you to lift heavy objects up than take them down from overhead, seriously consider lower cabinet plate and bowl storage.

A full depth drawer is a sure sign of quality and gives space you need.

Photo courtesy of KraftMaid

Drawers

If the drawers look like they are flimsy, cheaply made and thrown together, you can bet the rest of the cabinet is too. If the drawer is strong, square and glides in and out of the cabinet effortlessly, you are dealing with a manufacturer who is proud of his product.

The drawer box should be double doweled or dovetailed, rather than stapled and glued. The stress on drawers is down, not side-to-side. Therefore, drawer side thickness is not as critical as shelving thickness. Nevertheless, drawer sides should be at least 1/2-inch to 3/4-inch thick. Drawer bottoms must be dadoed into all four of the drawer's sides. Drawer bottoms and the drawer glides should be rated to hold at least 75-pounds.

The drawer with the heaviest load in your kitchen is probably the silverware drawer. The contents of a silverware drawer usually weighs 30 to 40-pounds. Rarely, a silverware drawer may hold 50-pounds. If the drawer in your cabinet is rated at 75-pounds, you have the security of knowing it will never be over burdened.

Drawer glides can be mounted on each side, or on the bottom. Some people find bottom-mounted drawer glides more attractive because they are invisible. A few manufacturers get by with a single glide mounted under the middle of the drawer. This is not acceptable.

From a practical point of view, side-mounted glides take a little bit of the useable width of the drawer. Bottom-mounted glides take a little bit of the useable height. No big deal either way. Whichever type of glide your drawers have, make certain that the glide system has a capture and hold mechanism, so you cannot accidentally pull the drawer off the glide. A loaded drawer dropping on your foot can cause serious injury. It will probably also break the drawer.

One often-overlooked area is how far the drawer extends into the depth of the cabinet. Most people look at a drawer and automatically believe that it goes all the way to the back. That is often not the case.

Cheap cabinets may have vanity drawers that only extend half the depth of the cabinet. Even many good cabinets only extend 3/4 of the way. Full-depth drawers are a sign of quality.

Photo courtesy of Merillat

Doors

Doors are usually solid wood or wood veneer. They come in four basic styles: raised panel, recessed panel, frame and panes, and flat panel.

Raised panels can be square, arched, or cathedral arch. Raised panel or sunken panel doors are made from a doorframe with center panels dadoed into the frame structure. Central panels are often very thin. The thicker the central panel, the firmer the door. Flat doors are solid pieces of wood or engineered wood with a vinyl or veneer outer skin. Glass mullion doors and leaded glass doors are also available.

Doors should have hidden, adjustable hinges that close automatically when the door is within 2 or 3 inches of the cabinet. This sounds like a little thing, but a slightly open door can be a safety hazard.

You should also know that hinges can open 90 degrees or 180 degrees. A hinge that just opens 90 degrees, could be a major drawback . Your best bet when cabinet shopping is to try to open the doors all the way.

Doors should also have bumpers at the bottom of the doorframe so that constant closing of the door does not wear away the surface of the cabinet frame or shelving.

Finish

The color of a cabinet is a design choice, so that is entirely your decision. The number of colors available and the quality of the finish definitely impacts the overall quality of the cabinet because it limits or expands your ability to get exactly what you want.

When you are in a showroom or at a builders' show, every cabinet you see looks good. All the major companies invest large amounts of money into getting and applying a superior finish. KraftMaid, as an example, advertises a 14-step furniture finish that beautifies and protects their doors, drawers and cabinets.

You are probably not an expert, so how do you tell the difference between the once over lightly and the multi-stage finish that will keep your cabinetry looking good for a long, long, time?

According to the experts at KraftMaid Cabinetry, the fastest way to tell the quality of a finish is to rub your hand lightly up and down on the door panels. If you feel any roughness or differences in texture, it is a sign of a bad finish.

The finish should not only look good, it should be strong enough to protect your cabinetry from all the household chemicals they are likely to come in contact with. To mention only a few, this includes gasoline, water, alcohol, fingernail polish, acetone, household soaps, Trisodium Phosphate, olive oil, citric acid, wax, crayon, tea, beet juice and vinegar.

You have every right to ask the salesman if the cabinet finish is strong enough to protect against all these chemicals and still look good.

Many cabinets, doors and drawers have had a vinyl or laminate applied to their exterior surface. This is fine. However, not every company has invested the money necessary for proper vinyl and laminate application. Merillat, as an example, uses a pressure-forming process that makes the outer layer adhere so tightly that it almost becomes an integral part of the inner structure. No matter how hard you try, you should only be able to see and feel one continuous surface. That's good.

Design features

Moldings are a "design choice" that says a great deal about cabinet quality. Crown and base moldings are the easiest way to give stock and semi-custom cabinets a "custom" look. If you don't have a broad selection of moldings available to you, the manufacturer, not you, has made the final decision. If you want the choice to be yours, shop elsewhere.

Having a wide selection of moldings lets you give semi-custom cabinets a custom look.

Photo courtesy of KraftMaid

Decorative hardware is another design option that helps you customize your kitchen.

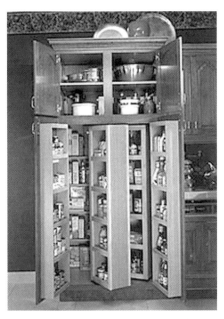

Some cabinet options like glass front drawer panels, spice boxes and stem glass holders are purely design choices. Other options, such as rollout trays, knife drawers with cutting boards, mixer shelves, multi-shelf pullout pantries, and lazy susans, are such work-savers they should almost be classed as necessities.

Having a wide variety of options is one of the keys to a functional kitchen. If your manufacturer doesn't make them available, you have to do without.

This KraftMaid pull out pantry tucks a lot of storeage space into what would normally be a very small cabinet area. Photo courtesy of KraftMaid

My advice: Look at all your options before you fall in love.

Company reputations

The most important test of cabinet quality is the reputation and dependability of the manufacturer, distributor and installer. Do they provide products in a timely manner? Do they provide replacements, if and when necessary? Can you get repairs in a timely manner? Do they stand behind their warranty?

If the cabinets you choose fill all these criteria, you can feel confident that you will have a kitchen that you will be pleased with for a long, long time.

28 Pick the right counter top for your lifestyle

Cabinetry by Timberlake Cabinet Company

Laminates

Laminates are the obvious best choice if you are updating the kitchen but not replacing cabinets, if you are redoing your kitchen as a do-it-yourself project, or if you are concerned with getting the lowest out-the-door cost. Laminates are made from a plastic veneer glued to particleboard. Formica, Nevamar and Wilsonart make the product in an almost inexhaustible number of colors.

Solid surface

Solid surface countertops are the second most popular and practical countertop material. First introduced in the 1960s, DuPont Corian and newer solid surface materials made by Wilsonart and Swanstone are made from acrylic and polyester materials. They can be either shiny or have a matte finish. Because they are a solid surface, a router can be used to carve drain boards or make distinctive edges. They are also very easy to care for.

High gloss, polished granite

High gloss, polished granite is today's dominant high-end kitchen countertop material. Granite comes in an infinite variety of colors and patterns from all over the world. Granite also combines beauty with strength and easy-care features. One of the newest looks in Granite is the "matte finish" look.

Most granites have to be sealed with a penetrating sealer before being used as a countertop. But once sealed, you shouldn't have to worry about spills or scratches. Even so, you still shouldn't cut on it or put a pan on it that is hotter than 350 degrees (the bottom of a pan just off the stove can be 650 degrees).

One word of caution. Thin granite and mass imported granite is making a big impression on the market and will definitely change the perceived value.

Composites

Scientists have been hard at work trying to do Mother Nature one better, and cheaper. For example, Silestone is a man-made stone that is 95 percent natural quartz and recycled glass and granite. Silestone is harder than granite, doesn't stain or absorb moisture, so no maintenance is required, and it has a 10-year replacement warranty. There are now many quartz composite countertop materials. They are becoming increasingly price competitive.

Honed limestone and soapstone

Honed limestone and soapstone are making inroads. Honed stone has a weathered mat finish. All natural stones have strengths and weaknesses inherent in the product. They may make a wonderful countertop but you have to learn to live with them and accept their characteristics.

Concrete

Concrete is gaining in popularity especially among kitchen designers who don't have to make it, live with it or take care of it. It is very heavy and most craftsmen still do not know how to work with it. Many homeowners hate the stress cracks.

Stainless steel

Stainless steel countertops are being used to compliment and extend the clean, efficient lines of commercial-look stainless steel appliances. Although stainless steel scratches and shows finger-prints, it is very easy to clean, and it is impervious to hot pans, oils and stains. Wood cabinetry can be used to soften the look for use in the home.

Pros and Cons of Countertop Materials

Surface	Heat resistance	Stain resistance	Scratch resistance
Concrete	Excellent	Fair	Good but no cutting
Granite	Good, nothing over 350 degrees	Excellent	Good but no cutting
Stainless steel	Excellent	Excellent	Good but no cutting
Corian and other solid surfaces	Not good, trivet suggested	Fair, most stains easily removed	Good but no cutting
Silestone and other quartz composites	Excellent	Excellent	Good but no cutting
Tile	Excellent	Tile good, grout bad	Good but no cutting
Laminate	Not good, trivet suggested	Good but not repairable	Good but not repairable

29 Cover the fundamentals and you'll have a great bathroom

Photo courtesy of Porcher / American Standard Inc.

On a square foot basis bathrooms are the most expensive rooms in the house. You can get as elaborate as you want. Here are some basics to get you started.

Reliable toilets
Toilets that do not flush properly are the Number 1 Complaint for new homebuilders. It has been that way ever since the federal legislation mandating low flush (1.6 gallons per flush) gravity feed toilets.

The first generation 1.6 toilets were an unmitigated disaster. Now many toilet manufacturers are on their fourth and fifth generation of toilets. Kohler, American Standard, Gerber, and Toto have all made great strides with their gravity feed toilets. Some cost $500 or more. Both Kohler and American Standard now claim that they have finally beaten the 1.6-gallon challenge. Prices on some of their new models are coming down.

As of this writing, the only 1.6 gallon toilets I can guaranty won't have a double flush problem are toilets that contain power flush mechanisms. The mechanisms are made by W.C. Technologies and Sloan Flushmate. These two companies sell their pressure valves to almost all the major toilet brand manufacturers. The manufacturers, in turn, sell pressure-assisted toilets.

Comfort
Score one for Universal Design. Many bathroom designers kept designing sleek, low designs. Very astute Kitchen and Bath designers like Mary Joe Peterson noticed that people over 35 actually found higher than average designs far more comfortable. The higher seat is easier to sit down on and get up.

In a shrewd marketing move, Kohler named the user-friendly design, comfort height, and included the design in many of their bath groupings. We can all sit easier.

Ease of use
For many years the Japanese manufacturer, Toto, has been at the cutting edge of toilet design. They now make an adjustable seat toilet with a built-in bidet.

American's are still very shy about discussing bidets and associate them only with feminine hygiene. Bidets were originally made to help both sexes clean up after a bowel movement. Toto's electrically powered system lets you adjust the bidet spray for a man's or woman's anatomy. You can also adjust the water pressure and temperature. The toilet, called the Washlet Chloe is expensive, but could go a long way toward helping an older or physically handicapped person use the toilet independently.

Shower design tips

There are really luxurious features you can build into your shower now, that will be lifesavers if you or a loved one is ever laid up. Design the shower with wide doors (or no doors) and zero clearance entry. This means that the entire bathroom floor be waterproof and that the bathroom have two drains, one in the shower, one in the bathroom proper so that any over spray goes down the drain instead of soaking into the floor.

Equip the shower with a seat, a shelf for soap and cleaning aids, and both a full body and a hand held showerhead. While you are at it, you might want to build in a steam bath. These features will make you feel spoiled now, but will also be indispensable aids if you or someone you love ever are wheelchair-bound, get arthritis or grow older.

If you are thinking about using glass block as a design feature, Pittsburgh Corning Glass Block has come out with walk-in shower glass block kits. The new kits come in three different glass block shower configurations.

The floor pans are specifically made for the shower configurations, virtually eliminating leaking. They are available through professional channels only. Give Pittsburgh Corning a call and see who is stocking them in your area.

Pre-Formed Accessible Showers

At the time of this writing there were six different manufacturers of accessible showers:

> **Swan** makes the barrier-free shower that complies with the Americans with Disabilities Act (ADA). The model number on the floor of the shower is BF-3060.

Sterling, a Kohler Company, makes this 63" accesible barrier-free, roll-in shower. They also make a 39" accessible trasfer shower with a roomy transfer seat. Photo courtesy of Sterling/a Kolhler Company

Lasco Bathware makes the ADA compliant shower, Model 1603-BFST.

Sterling makes a 63" Roll-In Shower, OC-S-63-ADA. Their parent company, **Kohler** makes the Freewill Barrier-Free Wheelchair Shower Module No. K-12102-P.

Both **Kohler** and **Bath Ease, Inc** make side opening whirlpool baths that make it easy for anyone who is wheelchair bound or has difficulty getting into and out of the bath.

Easy to Install Grab Bars

Many accidents are caused because the bar a person grabs onto for support either is not strong enough to bear the weight or the fastening system does not have the ability to anchor the bar solidly. Most grab bar fastening systems will pull out of the wall if they are not firmly anchored to the 2 X 4 or other heavy support behind the wall.

A relatively new grab bar fastening system called Wingits was created to give grab bars the extra support they need without being attached to a 2 X 4. Two fasteners cost $50 but support up to 350 pounds. The company also makes a complete selection of grab bars.

If you already have purchased a grab bar from another manufacturer, tell them the make and model number so that they can provide the proper-sized fastener.

Bathtub Replacement
There are really three options: *reglaze, replace, or reline*.

Reglazing is too delicate. It is an inexpensive fix but most people scratch off the glazing with normal use or cleaning. Rustoleum Tub & Tile Refinisher Epoxy Acrylic Paint advertises that their test models have withstood razor cuts and 1,000 hours of continuous fillings with very hot water.

Replacing gets expensive. If you have one of the old cast iron tubs the contractor usually has to cut it apart in the bathroom to even get it out of there.

My favorite alternative is *relining* the bathtub. They have been doing this in the hotel/motel industry for a half-century. Bathtub Reliners can make your bathtub look like new for less than half the cost of a remodel with an acrylic bath liner. As in most trades, some reliners are better than others so be sure to check references.

30   Basement remodeling is a bargain

Photo courtesy of Owens Corning

If you have a basement and need extra living, office or entertainment space, basement remodeling is the biggest bargain on the block. On a square footage basis, adding a room addition or a dormer will cost four or five times as much as remodeling the basement.

Be sure the basement is dry
If you are considering remodeling the basement, a thorough inspection is in order. Should there be any question of leaks in the basement, get the problem solved permanently before you invest money in remodeling.

In some instances it may pay to have the basement waterproofed, not damp proofed, from the outside, before you begin work.

Even if you have a "dry" basement, have a back flow preventer installed in the main drain so that water doesn't backup into your basement during a heavy rain.

The average house with poured basement walls has 180-rod holes. Any that are improperly sealed can develop leaks. Mr. Sponge has developed a unique do-it-yourself Rod Hole Patching Kit. Unfortunately the kit has only a very small amount of retail distribution but you can call the company at (800) 491-4686 and buy direct.

Stress cracks in the slab floor are very common and usually mean nothing. Major cracks, especially when one side is higher than the other or when the crack is widening, are an indication that there is a major shift of the ground beneath the slab. This is often caused by a subterranean flow of water and cannot be fixed from inside the house.

The final step to make sure you have worry-free walls is to coat them with a water stop. If the basement walls have not been previously painted, they can be coated with Xypex - HD-150, crystallizing water-proofing coating. The crystalline coating will actually penetrate the concrete and seal hairline cracks. It has been tested to stop up to 123 pounds of water pressure per square inch (PSI). I will tell you more about HD-150 later in this chapter.

Back up sump pumps a must

If the basement has a sump pump and your house is serviced by city water so there is always sufficient water pressure, install a water-powered back up sump pump. The Saginaw Pump Guardian by A. Y. McDonald is one of the better ones.

Battery powered back up sump pumps are also available but a battery only runs for 12 to 24 hours before it needs to be recharged. A really bad power outage can last for days. Once the battery runs out of power the back up pump it powers is useless. A water-powered back up sump pump will run as long as the city water lines have water pressure.

Make the basement safe

It is now code in many states that if you are going to use the basement for more than storage and a place to put the furnace and washing machine, you need an egress window. That means that if you are going to have children playing in the basement or use the area for an office or entertainment, you have another way to get out of the basement.

You should also have mandatory fire escape drills to teach the kids or anyone who might get caught in a basement fire how to open and use the egress window. The kids will think it is a fun game and it could easily save their lives.

Egress windows

Egress windows have to be big enough to crawl through and easy to get to. In Michigan that means that they must have 5.7 square feet of openable space with a minimum height of 24" and a minimum width of 20." The interior sill height can not be more than 44" above the floor. It should open up into a well that extends at least 36" from the face of the building. The well can not be more than 44" deep unless a ladder is installed that does not encroach more than 6" into the well.

The Bilco Scape Well has stairs that double as planters so egress is both easy and attractive. Photo courtesy of the Bilco Company

The installation of egress windows requires a professional, but if you want to learn all about the procedure, West Michigan Glass Block has photos plus step-by-step installation instructions on their web site, www.wmgb.com.

The Bilco Scape Well Window Well System and the Ag-Co Products Egress Window-Well System both turn a sunken window well into a flower planter that also serves as an emergency fire escape.

Seal and insulate walls to keep them dry and warm

Most basement remodeling contractors just insulate untreated basement walls. Sealing the surface before the studs and insulation are in place gives you extra security and can stop a lot of problems before they start.

If the basement walls have not been previously painted, they can be coated with Xypex - HD-150, crystallizing waterproofing coating. The crystalline coating will actually penetrate the concrete and seal hairline cracks. It has been tested to stop up to 123 pounds of water pressure per square inch (PSI). This is 12 times the water stopping power of any other product I know of and 24 times the industry average.

The only problem with the Xypex coating is that it can only be applied to raw concrete. If you have ever sealed the concrete or applied a waterproofing paint, you are out of luck.

Two new basement paints have recently been added to the Do-It-Yourselfer's arsenal. Both block water and, just as important, fight the mold often associated with damp basement conditions. Wm. Zinsser has introduced WaterTite Mold and Mildew-Proof Water-proofing Paint. The paint will stop 10 pounds of water pressure, which is twice as much as most brands. It also contains ingredients that will keep mold or mildew from growing on the paint surface for 5 years.

DAP has introduced Kwik Seal Plus Basement Paint with Microban. The Microban technology is what makes this a break-through paint. Microban treated products kill microbials on contact. That means that the mold and mildew protection is provided between the paint film and the concrete wall as well as on the dried painted surface.

After the walls have been sealed it is time to insulate the concrete and attach the wall system. There are several different methods of doing this. Depending upon the amount of insulation you choose to install, you can use furring strips, 2 x 4s, or steel 2 x 4s. Steel weighs less and is easier to work with.

Dow makes Wallmate, a special slotted Styrofoam insulation for basement walls. It can be laid directly against the concrete and attached by 1-by-3 furring strips, which are also used for hanging the drywall. Wallmate comes in a 1-1/2 inch thickness providing 7.5 R-value and a 2-inch thickness providing 10 R-value.

If you want more insulation, you can frame the walls with either wood or steel 2 x 4s and use fiberglass batts. Owens Corning recommends 3-1/2-inch batts of Miraflex in "itch free" perforated poly wrap. This provides an R-Value of R-13.

Don't forget to caulk and insulate the band joists. In a well-insulated house, up to 30 percent of heat loss can often be traced to uninsulated band joists.

The Delta FL dimpled waterproofing membrane creates an air space between the concrete floor and the floor above. Photo courtesy of Cosella Dorken.

Best Type Of Wall Sheathing For Basements

Once the insulation is installed, it is time to hang the sheathing. Paneling has to be part of the definition of the term "rec room." Today the very sight of paneling in a downstairs living or office area says "throw-away" space.

Photo courtesy of Coy Construction

Drywall is my favorite basement wall and ceiling material. The reasons I like it are that it makes basement rooms look more like the rest of the house and it is easy to put up and inexpensive enough to tear out if it gets wet. I recommend always using Moisture Resistant (MR) drywall below grade. It costs a little more, but is far less moisture-sensitive than regular drywall.

Owens Corning has developed a truly excellent proprietary wall material specifically for basement remodeling that is mold and damp proof. The panels are made from 2-1/2-inch thick rigid fiberglass covered with fiberglass. They are mold and moisture resistant and provide an insulation factor of R-11.

The Owens Corning product is not available everywhere and is sold and installed exclusively through licensed dealers, not the general public. However, if you are going to have your basement remodeled, you should learn if there is a dealer in your area and take a look at the system.

Make the basement look like the rest of the house
Mike McCoy, of Coy Construction Inc., one of the biggest basement remodeling specialists in the country, gives the following 6 tips to make your basement look and feel like living space:

1. Remove the basement door and at least one of the walls enclosing the basement stairway. This will open up the first floor and permit the living area to flow down to the lower level gracefully. The only reason the builder put a wall at the top of the basement stairs was to save money by not finishing off the basement.

2. Carpet the basement stairs and the basement floor with carpeting that is at least as good as that in the living room.

3. If you have a two-story house, the banister on the stairway wall leading down to the basement should be as good or better quality than the banister leading up to the second floor.

4. Install picture windows between basement rooms so that you never get a "locked in" feeling.

5. Make certain that there is plenty of light. Use recessed lighting wherever possible so that the ceilings can be as high as possible.

6. Use light colored paint and wallpaper to brighten the basement and make it feel light and airy.

Basement Flooring

As long as the basement is dry, you can do anything you would or could do anywhere else including vinyl sheet goods, vinyl or ceramic tile, carpeting, wood or laminate. You do this with the understanding that if wood or laminate flooring gets wet, they are usually ruined. If there is standing water on carpeting for any length of time, it should be thrown away. At a minimum, wet padding must be torn out and discarded.

The Envira Cushion imported and distributed by Fairway Tile and Carpet is the only carpet padding I know that has a 4.5 R factor so it makes the floor warmer. It is also waterproof, odorless, nontoxic and even impervious to dog and cat urine. You couldn't do better in the basement if you are going to lay carpeting.

Cosella Dorken has introduced Delta-FL, a dimpled sub floor sheeting that uses air-gap technology to insulate and protect the basement floor from cold, damp and minor leaks. It is scientifically engineered to keep moisture from passing through the concrete slab into living space. It was designed for laminate flooring but can also be used with hardwood, carpet and vinyl sheeting.

31 How to waterproof a basement

According to statistics developed by Cosella-Doerken, a worldwide manufacturer of waterproofing materials, only one home in 5,000 is ever hit by fire and just one home in 250 is burglarized; but one in 8 homes experiences basement leaks and water damage not covered by insurance!

This statistic is limited to major water damage. It does not even consider the potential building and medical damage caused by moisture wicked up into building walls from damp basements.

If a basement is not waterproofed, it is just a hole in the ground waiting to fill with water. Builders know this but most just damp-proof basements because it's cheaper.

If you already have a water problem or want to convert your basement to living or even quality storage space, it should be waterproofed.

Different types of waterproofing systems
There is a new (for the United States), high-tech solution coming on stream that has me very excited if it works as advertised. A Wisconsin company called Drytronic Inc. markets and installs a unique patented technology that permanently stops water intrusion and reduces high humidity in most at or below grade concrete structures.

This is not a coating. The Electro-Osmotic Pulse (EOP) System uses an electronic pulse to create a reverse osmosis condition in the concrete which causes water to go from the inside, out, instead of from the outside, in.

The dewatering concept was developed in Europe during the 1980s, and has been used successfully on a number of US government installations. It can be installed effectively even when the concrete has previously been painted. Once the installation has been made the US distributor says that it will not cost more than a 70-Watt light bulb to operate.

The Drytronic system sounds very exciting. The only problem is that the company seems to be having difficulty setting up its US distribution network. If you are interested in learning more, call Drytronic and see if there is a dealer in your area.

Other than the Drytronic system the only way to truly waterproof a basement is from the outside. This is best done when the house is being built.

A waterproof membrane, such as Tremco Barrier Solutions' Tuff-N-Dri, can be sprayed onto the concrete followed by an insulating board that both insulates the concrete from external ground temperature and helps to drain away moisture.

The Cosella Doerken Delta-DL system adds a Dimpled Plastic Water Barrier that channels water down to the drain vents and protects the concrete walls from roots or other outside influences.

On an existing house they have to dig all the way down to the footers and install an impermeable waterproof membrane of some kind. When this is done, a new drainage system is also installed.

One of the major causes of water in basements is that the drainage tiles designed to take water away from the basement have collapsed or clogged. When this happens, trenches can be dug around the walls and new tile and waterproofing installed on the exterior walls of the basement. This is very expensive and disruptive to landscaping.

The problem can also be solved from the inside through the installation of an interior drain tile system or a re-channeling system.

Interior Drain Tile System
If you choose the interior drain tile system, the slab will be cut and a complete new set of PVC drains protected by a fiberglass filter fabric, and gravel or crushed stone are laid below the slab along the inside wall. Clean outs are installed so that the drainpipes can be snaked out. Drain water collects in the PVC pipe through holes in the bottom of the pipes and is routed to the sump pump or city storm sewer.

The benefit of this system is that the water is collected underneath the slab. Once the "fix" has been put in place the concrete is patched so that the integrity of the slab is maintained.

Re-Channeling System

A re-channeling system drains the basement walls through holes drilled at the base of the wall. Water drained from the walls is collected and channeled by a hollow plastic molding which directs the water into the sump pump.

The Combination Approach
A new technique that is being introduced by Basement Systems, Inc. and their dealer group throughout the US and Canada. The technique consists of installing Cosella-Doerken's Delta-MS on the walls of damp basements and channeling the moisture into drainage channels. The Delta-MS can then be drywalled and provide a perfectly dry wall surface.

I am not recommending any one of these systems as being better than the others. They are all expensive and they all would be unnecessary if your builder had done the right thing and drywalled your basement in the first place.

32 Don't choose flooring on looks alone

Vinyl, Laminate or Hardwood?

A good vinyl, laminate or hardwood flooring can all look like wood. The difference is that vinyl and laminate are pictures of wood and hardwood is the real thing.

Vinyl is the most obvious photograph. It is a sheet that is spread across the floor. Because it is a solid surface it is impervious to surface moisture. Spill some water and mop it up right away and there is no harm done. Vinyl is the epitome of the easy care surface.

A laminated surface looks good. It stands up to traffic and is easy to clean with a damp mop. But it is not for everyone. Retailers keep telling me about customers who buy laminate, then have it yanked out because they can't live with it.

Wood is the real thing. It looks and sounds different from laminate and is far more durable. A wood floor is considered "life of structure." Laminate and vinyl are not.

Laminated flooring is like paint. You use it to make a statement. If you don't like the color of your walls, you put on another coat of paint. If you change your mind about the look of laminated flooring, tear it out and put in something new.

Laminate is a good, long wearing flooring. It is highly sensitive to moisture and many people are put off by the "clip clop" sound that results when you walk over it.

Most good vinyl flooring has to be installed by professionals to maintain the warranty. On the other hand, laminated flooring manufactures do everything they can to make installing laminated flooring an easy Do-It-Yourself project. The new "click in," no glue floating laminate flooring is exceptionally easy to install. You can find step-by-step installation guides on most manufacturer's web sites.

Hardwood can be installed by an advanced Do-It-Yourselfer. It is usually installed by a professional.

33 Choose the carpeting for your lifestyle

When you go into a carpet store the choices are mind-boggling. But what is right for your house, your family, your life-style? Here's a short guide to give you some direction before you even go into the store.

Remember when you set out to buy carpeting, you are really buying three things: carpet, padding, and installation. This means that the quality of the store is as important as the quality of the carpeting. If the store does not have good padding or good installers, it doesn't matter how good a price you get, you are going to be unhappy.

Most carpeting is nylon
Roughly 97 percent of all carpeting is made from synthetic fibers. Two thirds of the carpeting in the U.S. is nylon. Nylon is very strong and can last almost forever. It holds colors very well and is quite stain resistant. Major manufacturers' branded nylons, like Monsanto Wear-Dated, Dupont Stainmaster, and Allied Anso, can be even better because they are especially "tweaked" to have specific features, like wear or stain resistance.

About 30 percent of the carpet fiber made is Olefin (polypropylene). It is very colorfast and easy to clean. Often used in indoor and outdoor carpeting, Olefin can cost up to 30 percent less than nylon.

Two other synthetics are polyester and acrylic. Polyester makes a very luxurious, thick pile carpet. Acrylic gives the appearance and feel of wool, without the price.

Wool — the great, natural carpet fiber — is very luxurious and durable. It hides dirt because of its light scattering characteristics. Unlike synthetic fibers, wool does not melt when exposed to fire, it chars. Wool makes a very high quality, but pricey, carpet.

Looped carpet fibers wear best
Carpeting comes in several different textures. With level loop piles, like Berbers, the yarn is looped at the top. Multi-level loop pile carpeting is merely looped carpeting with two or three different loop heights. Looped carpeting is excellent for high traffic areas because it shows wear very slowly. Foot traffic is on top of the loop, which is really the side of the fiber.

Because they bear up to traffic so well, Berbers are very good for family rooms, halls and stairways. They are also an excellent choice when you want the entire house to have the same carpeting.

In plush pile carpeting, the top of the loops are cut off. The most popular are Velvets and Saxonies.

Velvets have very smooth, luxurious surfaces. They show foot traffic because the areas that are walked on lean to one side and reflect light differently from the rest of the carpet.

In a textured Saxony weave, the top of the yarn is cut at different angles so that traffic and wear patterns are not as noticeable.

Cut pile carpeting is best for low traffic rooms like bedrooms, living rooms, and dining rooms.

A textured carpeting called Frieze combines the strength of a level loop pile with the look of a plush pile. A Frieze carpet has had the top of the loop cut off, but the top of the yarn is then crimped over to one side so that you get almost the same wear characteristics as Berber.

There are also various textured and cut and loop combinations and patterns but these specialized weaves take only a very small proportion of carpeting sales.

Beige is the most popular carpet color

There isn't a man alive who is going to win an argument about color with his wife or girlfriend. Even though 65 percent of all carpeting sold is beige, if you are a man and a rebellious "non-beiger," here's how to sound intelligent while you lose.

According to the professionals, light colors open up a room and make it look larger. They also show footprints less. Dark colors make a room seem warmer and cozier. Dark and multi-colored carpets are also good at hiding soils and stains.

Expensive carpet fiber does not reflect light

Check the highlights of the yarn. Higher quality yarns reflect less light. The higher the quality, the duller the carpeting will be. Shiny carpet yarns accentuate defects. They show footprints and soiling more than dull carpets.

Another way to tell inexpensive from better carpeting is to make a close-up inspection of the fibers. The thinner and more tightly packed the threads, the better the carpet. If all else fails, turn the carpeting sample over. Better quality carpet will have both the name of the chemical company that produced the yarn, usually Mannington, DuPont, BASF, or Allied, in addition to the name of the mill that actually wove the carpet.

Carpeting experts tell me that if the name of the chemical company is on the sample, both the mill and the chemical company are standing behind the warranty. If only the mill's name is on the carpet, only the mill is standing behind the warranty.

Quality padding is just as important as quality carpeting

The padding under the carpet is so important that installing an improper cushion can void the warranty.

The five most common types of padding are synthetic hair, prime Urethane, rebond Urethane, flat rubber and ripple rubber.

Prime Urethane is very good but expensive. Unlike a fine wine, you are not going to impress anyone, even the carpeting, by ordering a prime Urethane. Consider it only if you are buying a very expensive wool.

Two excellent types of padding are synthetic hair and rebond Urethane. They commonly come in 2-, 4-, 6-, and 8-pound weights. Eight-pound padding is the best and well worth the money for heavy traffic areas. Six-pound padding is the most popular. Going below 6-pound will effect the wear and feel of the carpet.

There are really three types of rubber padding: flat, rippled, and bubble rubber. Flat and rippled rubber are excellent. They are waterproof and often used in basements and other cement slab installations.

Bubble rubber padding does not have sufficient density and thickness and can cause premature aging of the carpet. Using it can void the manufacturer's warranty.

If you are going to install carpeting on a concrete slab or in the basement and want a warmer floor, consider the Envira Cushion imported from Mexico by Fairway Tile & Carpet. It is environmentally friendly, waterproof, and lists an R factor of 4.5. If you don't like cold feet, it is worth the premium.

Expert installation is critical
No matter what the lady or gentleman at a big box store tries to tell you, do not try to install the carpet and padding yourself. Expert installation is so important that amateur installation often voids the carpet warranty.

You can usually save one dollar a yard by moving the furniture yourself and another dollar a yard by pulling up the old carpeting. Do not remove the old carpet tack strips. Tearing them out can ruin the wood underneath. Besides, the older strips are wider and better than those with which they would be replaced.

Removing the old carpeting yourself is a good idea for a couple of reasons. First, you get to give the floor a thorough cleaning and can make any necessary repairs. Second, you can fix any squeaks in the floor before the carpeting goes down.

34   The right window depends upon your needs and neighborhood

The best window is the one that is installed correctly. That being said the best windows for your home are the ones that fit in with the neighborhood, are energy efficient and easy to use.

Quality installation is critical
Ask the installers you are interviewing for customer referrals. Call the customers and find out if they were happy. Better still, ask them if you can drive by their house and take a look at the window job. If they like the job, they'll be glad to brag about it. If not, you learned a great deal about the installer.

There are many excellent window manufacturers. Some are large national companies like Andersen, St. James Co., Kolbe & Kolbe Millwork, Marvin, Pella, Traco. Some are local manufacturers like Wallside, Weather Shield, and Weathergard in the Detroit Area.

If you find a really good contractor, you can rely on his expertise and feeling of self-worth to know that he will choose what he believes to be a really top-notch window manufacturer. If you choose a bad contractor, you will be unhappy no matter how good the window he installs.

The best window for your house depends upon the neighborhood. If most of the homeowners are replacing their windows with wood framed windows, you should do the same. If most of the folks are replacing their old windows with vinyl, you can do the same thing and save a lot of money.

Let's start by admitting that having wood framed windows have always been considered a sign of quality. Wood frames can be beautifully finished. They can be easily painted and repainted to match your décor. Composite, fiberglass and vinyl can be laminated to look like wood. Renewal composite windows by Andersen are often laminated with a true wood veneer that can even be stained or painted.

Whether you choose solid wood or wood-framed windows clad with aluminum or vinyl is a personal choice. Solid wood frames have to be painted or stained on a regular basis. Vinyl- or aluminum-clad (covered wood) frames do not. The slight difference in the R-value (resistance to heat flow) between the four different styles is not enough to affect your decision.

Composite, fiberglass and metal-framed windows can last, practically, forever. Vinyl framing is softer, but still has very good wear characteristics. Many of the wood framed windows in historic houses are more than 100 years old when replaced.

Cheap "builder quality" wood windows like those found in many new homes often have to be replaced within 7 years.

Although most of the windows in commercial buildings are aluminum framed, their frames are very inefficient when it comes to insulation value.

All that being said, windows are considered 25-year replacement items. You will probably not live in your present house more than ten years. Few houses are standing after 100 years. Do you really care if a window frame can last 200 years?

The biggest problem some people have with vinyl-framed windows is that they usually have wider frames than wood windows. This can be especially apparent if you have small windows. The problem is called the "port hole" effect. It is one of the reasons why you should never buy from a salesman's sample. Always check full sized windows and look at previously installed windows before you buy.

Good windows are tested to make it easy to determine quality
The better the glass, the better the window. Many windows are rated by the National Fenestration Rating Council (NFRC). The NFRC rates windows for U-Factor, Solar Heat Gain, and Visible Transmittance, and air leakage. Compare the ratings and you can decide which window will perform the best. If a window has been tested, it will have an NFRC label on the window showing rating results.

Windows, which perform to a high enough standard, receive an Energy Star label. There are different requirements for different parts of the country.

Any window with an Energy Star label is a good window. Compare the NFRC ratings to determine which is best.

The NFRC label appears on all products certified to NFRC standards and on all windows that are part of the Energy Star program.

The NFRC label shows the windows U-Factor, Solar Heat Gain (SHGC), Visible Transmittance (VT) and Air Leakage (AL).

The U-Factor measures the way the window transmits heat created from sources other than the sun. It tells how effective a window is at keeping the outside temperature outside and the inside temperature inside. The lower the U-Factor, the less energy goes through the window.

Here are recommendations for the ratings you should look for in the Northern tier of states.

A U-Factor of .32 is better than a U-Factor of .50. You shouldn't buy a window with a U-Factor above .35. Some triple paned windows have U-Factors as low as .15.

Solar Heat Gain Coefficient measures the way a window absorbs heat from the sun, the lower the better. A .45 rating is better than a .60. If cooling is important, choose windows with an SHGC of .54 or below.

Visible Transmittance measure the percentage of visible light that comes through the product. The higher the VT, the better the view. A .60 VT is better than .54.

Air Leakage (AL) is a relatively new rating criteria. Your best choice in windows is .3 or lower.

Here is a listing of the recommended NFRC ratings for the three zones.

Zone	U-FACTOR	SHGC	VT	AL
Northern Zone	.35 or lower	.54 or lower	The higher the better	.3 or lower
Central Zone	.40 or lower	.40 or lower	The higher the better	.3 or lower
Southern Zone	.60 or lower	.40 or lower	The higher the better	.3 or lower

Finally, a good window is one you can use

The reason we have just discussed the nuts and bolts of windows, not their styles is that most people consider style a design element. If you are comparing double hung windows and use the criteria discussed in this tip, you can easily decide which is your best double hung window choice. It is the same for casement or sliding windows.

If you close your eyes and if I say the word "window" you will probably visualize a double hung window. They are the standard for the majority of residential window applications in the United States.

Unfortunately when you open a double hung window you are lifting the lower half of the window. That window becomes increasingly hard to open over the years. If you are not particularly strong or over 60-years of age, the window may well be impossible for you to raise, or once raised, lower sufficiently to lock.

This is not a problem if you don't want to open your windows. If you want to be able to open to let in fresh air and close and lock windows to shut out both cold breezes and bad guys you have to have windows you can use.

The easiest to use windows are casement (opened by rotating a handle), gliding windows such as sliders (a window opening side to side instead of up and down), and hinged hopper windows (open out like a spout and are pulled back in).

These windows often require a different opening than a double hung window, but should be included if you like fresh air and want to age in place and comfort.

35 The right deck depends on how much work you want to do

Wooden decks are like wooden boats, beautiful but a maintenance nightmare. The only people who actually like to varnish wood are boat owners, and they invented fiberglass.

There are decking alternatives that only need no maintenance except an occasional cleaning. These materials made from plastic/ wood composites, virgin plastic and vinyl are more expensive than most wood decks but let you use the deck for what it was designed: relaxation.

At present all decks require a pressure treated wood understructure. The horizontal deck surface and rail systems can be made from any wood or non-wood decking material.

I have listed a representative sample of non-wood choices. This is not a comprehensive listing because new decking materials are constantly being introduced.

Extruded composites

These include Trex, the granddaddy of them all, ChoiceDek, and newer entries like Monarch, Smart Deck Durawood EX and TimberTech. Extruded wood composites are used for decking not understructures. All are almost impervious to insect and weather damage.

All composite decking materials turn gray from the sun but do not require staining or sealing. Once sealed, however, they require the same maintenance schedule as wood. Performance Coatings makes Knotwood Penofin a sealer especially made for composite decking.

Trex, made by the Trex Company is a combination of ground-up plastic milk cartons and wood waste. It is smooth and solid. You cut and nail it like wood decking. You can also use it to build the deck rail system. It never splits or rots. The biggest disadvantages of Trex is that it looks exactly like what it is — a semi/plastic extrusion. It is slightly moisture absorbent. Trex will take a solid stain, but then you are back into the maintenance thing. My advice is to let it weather light gray.

ChoiceDek, manufactured by AERT (Advanced Environmental Recycling Technologies, Inc.), is a 100-percent recycled-content, wood-plastic composite decking material distributed in some parts of the country by Weyerhaeuser.

ChoiceDek is dark brown when installed, but weathers to silver gray. Unlike Trex, ChoiceDek has a corrugated bottom surface. ChoiceDek also has a rough, non-slip surface.

Durawood EX is a wood fiber/polymer composite made from 70-percent recycled wood waste and 30-percent recycled milk jugs. It is part of the SmartDeck system made by Chicago-based Eaglebrook Products. EX is manufactured in continuous extrusions up to 12 inches wide. The type of wood fiber used in the manufacturing process determines coloring.

Eaglebrook also make Durawood PE a 100 percent-purified plastic lumber. PE comes in various wood tones and in popular colors such as cedar, weathered redwood, light oak, gray, white, green, dark brown, black, and custom colors and comes in most lumber sizes. It cannot be painted.

Monarch Composite Decking is made by Green Tree Composites, LLC is solid and comes in standard lumber dimensions so that it can be installed just like wood decking. It comes in cedar, red-wood, steel and driftwood colors and can be painted.

TimberTech is made from virgin, not recycled, plastics and wood fiber. Even though it is as strong as solid deck board, it is made with a hollow core and is bottomless. This makes it lighter and easy to string electrical wiring for on-deck lighting. The product has a nonskid surface, comes in 6-inch widths that fit tongue in groove. It can be stained, but weathers to a nice driftwood shade.

Plastic decking

100% plastic can be very beautiful. I do not know how it will hold up to the elements long term. There are also some concerns that it can be quite slippery when wet. Eon by CPI Plastics is a virgin plastic decking material that looks like beautiful hardwood.

Vinyl decking

Vinyl decking's biggest plus and minus is the same. It looks like plastic. That said, it could make a beautiful deck. If you buy vinyl, make certain that it has been treated to resist Ultra Violet rays to keep the material from becoming brittle.

Although there may be some fading from the sun, the color you buy is the color you keep. This makes Vinyl an excellent combination of long life, good looks and easy care.

The product comes from the dock and fencing industries. Some of the names to look for are:

> *Brock Deck,* built by a division of Royal Crown Ltd. Planks are 5-7/8 inches wide.

> *DreamDeck* by Thermal Industries. Planks are 5-1/2 inches wide.

> *EZ Deck* by Pultronex Corporation. Planks are 4 or 6 inches wide.

> *Kroy's Vinyl Decking* by Kroy Building Products. Planks are 8 inches wide.

The Brock Deck and EZ Deck have bottomless construction. All four have their own railing and attachment systems.

All hope is not lost if you already have a wooden deck

If you already have a wood deck but are not happy with the constant maintenance, you have two alternatives.

Cover the old

Durable Deck by Anchor Decking Systems, Inc. can be applied over your existing decking to provide a long-lasting, skid resistant cap.

You can also cover it with products like Versa Dek, a single Ply PVC waterproof membrane by Versa Dek Industries, or build a multi-step high performance coating like Versa Deck – Plus, by Versatile Building Products.

Tear off the old or start new

If you do not like the choice of materials offered for covering decks, you can usually tear off the old decking and cover the existing understructure with the composite, plastic or vinyl decking materials I listed at the top of this tip.

36 Follow these rules to take the "con" out of concrete

Most concrete driveways look good when they are one week old. Some last for 35 to 50 years. Some scale rapidly and start looking terrible within the first year. If you pick a good contractor and don't beat him to death on price, you'll get a good job. For those willing to be a little more technical, there are ways to make certain that you get a better than average job.

Preparation

As it is with every home improvement, proper preparation is the most important step. The sub grade should be uniform compacted sand or gravel. Some contractors prefer to compact the existing soil. This is not a good idea because you do not know what foreign elements may be in existing soil. The sand or gravel will be completely uniform. This uniform foundation actually strengthens the concrete, so it adds to the value of your job.

Drainage

Proper drainage is key to the longevity of concrete. The grade of a drive should be sloped a minimum of 1/8th of an inch per foot from all existing structures. Adjoining grass should slope a minimum of 1/2-inch toward the drive and away from the structures. Staked forms should outline the course of the drive.

Mix

Steve Klochko, Gibraltar National, knows more about concrete than anyone else I know. Klochko says that it is very important to specify the exact quality of concrete you want used on your driveway. He recommends a six-bag mix with a 3-inch slump. Properly cured, this concrete mix will develop a PSI OF 3,600 to 4,000 pounds.

In the days before cement trucks, Portland cement would be transported in 94-pound bags. A six-bag mix means that there are 564 pounds of Portland cement per cubic yard of concrete.

A stiff slump makes a good job

Slump is the way the amount of water in the mix is measured. Klochko says that a 3-inch slump is a very stiff mix, very hard work for the crew and gives you a stronger drive. A 4 or 5-inch slump is easier on the contractor's crew, but gives you less quality.

You will have a choice of a 4 or 5-inch thick slab. A 5-inch slab costs more, but is far stronger. You also may want to strengthen the slab. Many people suggest fiber. Klochko says that fiber is an excellent strengthening agent when resurfacing or repairing concrete. When pouring concrete, metal mesh adds greater strength and longevity.

Tricks of the trade that can cost you money

As in all businesses, slight of hand is very common and you have to be on the lookout to make certain that the cement truck driver and the contractor's crew do not pull the wool over you eyes. Even though it is on the contract, be sure to tell both the driver of the cement truck and the head of the contractor's crew that you require a 3-inch slump job.

Make your comments right before the cement truck driver begins to pour the concrete. If you are not on the alert, there is a strong possibility that the crew foreman may signal the driver to start adding water to the mix. The added water will make it faster and easier for the crew, but changes the concrete from a 3 to a 4-inch slump, decreasing the strength and quality of the concrete.

The one exception to the "No water added" policy is that on a particularly hot day, the concrete may begin to overheat in the truck. Water has to be added to make the concrete pour properly.

After the concrete is poured, the crew should begin to finish the drive as soon as all the standing water has disappeared. This means that the crew will have to wait about 40 minutes between the pour and finishing.

Finishing

When the slab is being finished, you should be careful not to let the foreman "bless" the new surface with water, Klochko warns. Blessing makes it easier for the workmen to finish, but severely lessens the integrity of the slab.

To assure strong curing, Klochko recommends using a product like Cure and Seal as soon as the surface is finished.

Joints

After finishing, the concrete should be grooved, or jointed. During this process, the surface is cut to a depth of no less than 1 inch to give room for the concrete to expand and contract. If the grooving is done by hand, it can be done as soon as the surface can be walked on. If done with a concrete saw, the procedure is delayed about 24 hours.

Joints should be spaced no more than 10 feet apart. When the slab is 12 feet or wider, a joint also should be cut down the center of the slab.

Curing
The concrete drive should then be left to cure for about seven days. After seven days, the drive may be driven on, but the concrete will continue to cure for a month or more.

Sealing
After 30 days, seal the concrete with a good silicone water-based sealer.

If you make sure that this is done, you should have a drive you will be bragging about for the next 30 years.

37 Here's the sticky on asphalt drives

All asphalt walks and drives are made of bituminous materials in what is called a hot mix. This mix is composed of stone, sand and the bituminous material that glues everything together.

The strength of the asphalt is determined by the size of the stones and the proportion of stone to sand to bituminous material. Installation is very specialized and requires heavy equipment.

The sub-base is key to the longevity of the job
Topsoil should be cleared and ground should be excavated to required depth. Soft spots need to be removed and replaced. Then the sub grade should be compacted to a smooth, free draining, even slope.

The thicker the base the better

The base should be made up of five or more inch depth of crushed stone, aggregate, highway gravel, recycled or crushed concrete. After the base has been compacted the actual asphalt can be laid.

Asphalt laid in two lifts

A good residential asphalt drive should be laid in two, two-inch thick lifts equaling four inches of asphalt on top of five inches of crushed stone.

The minimum acceptable would be two, 1-1/2-inch thick lifts equaling a three-inch pad of asphalt laid on top of five inches of crushed stone.

As a general rule, the thickness of the lift is double that of the largest stones in the mix. A two-inch lift therefore has one-inch diameter stones. If you only get a 1-1/2-inch lift, the largest stones have a diameter of only 3/4-inch, quite often only 5/8-inch diameter stones.

Larger stones and a thicker lift give a better job

Remember, the larger the stones, the thicker the lift, the longer lasting the job. You will get many extra years out of the higher priced, thicker product.

When the job is finished, you may see some stones showing in the drive. A stone showing just means that two stones landed on top of each other when pushed into place. It is not a defect. Do not pull out the stones because doing so could ruin the integrity of the asphalt.

After the driveway has been laid, you can wait for a year before sealing. When you seal the drive be sure to use a good asphalt emulsion sealer.

Chapter III
Major Home Systems

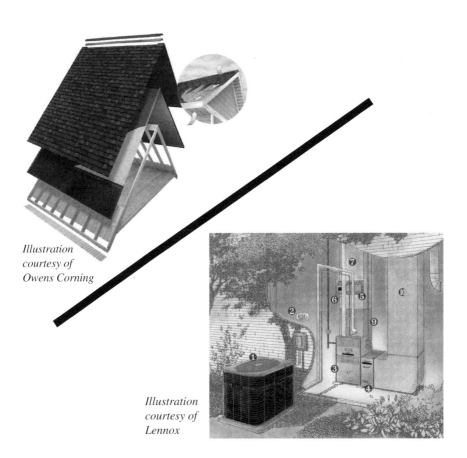

Illustration courtesy of Owens Corning

Illustration courtesy of Lennox

Heating, Cooling, Ventilation and Air Quality

38 Optimum heating, cooling and air quality require an integrated system

Imagine the car you would have if you bought the engine from Ford, the transmission from Chevrolet, the seats from Chrysler, the brakes from Honda, the frame from Fiat, the windows from Toyota and the steering from Isuzu. Then you called in an independent contractor and told him to jury-rig the parts together and put some kind of a body around the thing.

Now compound the problem by using the lowest bid basis for selection and not bother to check the references.

If you had a car like that, I can assure you of two things: You would never get me in the passenger seat, and I would try my darndest not to be on the same road with you.

You, of course, would never buy a car like that and if you did, the government would never let you put it on the road.

Unfortunately this is exactly the way most of our HVAC (Heating, Venting, Air Conditioning) systems are put together. Is it any wonder that most of us live in homes that are too hot in summer, too cold in winter and unhealthy and energy inefficient most of the time?

Listeners and readers come to me all the time wanting recommendations on furnaces, air conditioners, humidifiers, filters, air handlers, thermostats, etc. What many fail to understand is that all this equipment is supposed to work together as an integrated system. Today's more sophisticated equipment is even more interdependent.

This Lennox illustration does a good job of showing how your furnace and air conditioner work together as an integrated system. The prime ingredients to that system are: 1- air conditioner, 2- thermostat, 3- furnace, 4- filter/air cleaner, 5- germicidal UV light, 6- humidifier, 7- air supply duct, 8- energy recovery unit or air makeup unit (not shown), 9- refrigerant coil and 10- return air duct. Illustration courtesy of Lennox Industries, © 2002.

Your home's heating will be far more efficient with the proper humidification. The effectiveness of the air conditioning is directly dependent upon the efficiency of the furnace blower motor. The efficiency of both the furnace and the air conditioner are related to the accuracy and sensitivity of the thermostat. The quality of your home's air and the comfort of its inhabitants are dependent upon your HVAC systems air cleaning and air makeup capability.

Every time you replace one of the components of the HVAC system you have an effect on the operating capability, efficiency and effectiveness of every other component in the system.

You can not possibly know the intricacies of every component in your HVAC system, but your HVAC contractor is supposed to know all about your entire system.

If you want to get the most value, efficiency and comfort for you heating and cooling dollar, do two things.

1. Your HVAC system is far more valuable to your family's health, happiness and comfort than the sum of its parts. Think of it as an integrated system. When it comes time to replace, take the systems approach and make certain that the various parts will work well together before you buy.

2. Even more important: be very careful in the selection of your HVAC contractor. Once you have found a good one, rely on him, confide in him and don't try to undercut him.

39 The best furnace

When listeners ask me what is the best furnace, my first answer is, was and will always be: The best furnace is the one that is installed correctly. Your furnace isn't sized or installed by the manufacturer. It is sized and installed by your Heating, Venting and Air Conditioning (HVAC) contractor. You will not call the manufacturer if anything goes wrong and the heat goes out in the middle of the night. You will call your HVAC contractor.

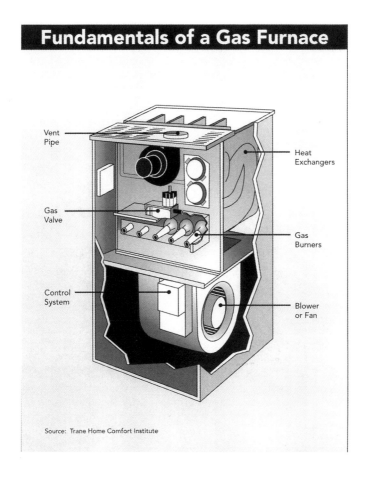

Fundamentals of a Gas Furnace

Vent Pipe

Heat Exchangers

Gas Valve

Gas Burners

Control System

Blower or Fan

Source: Trane Home Comfort Institute

A run of the mill furnace selected after a thorough heat loss study, engineered, installed and lovingly maintained by an excellent HVAC technician will give you excellent service. The best furnace in the world, engineered, installed and sloppily maintained by some bozo who would rather be someplace else and just wants your money, will give you nothing but problems.

At the same time, the top technicians and contractors gravitate to the best manufacturers because they know that their reputation is riding on every installation. They want to represent, sell and install equipment they can be proud of. Quality people gravitate toward quality companies. It is that simple.

One measure of quality is the efficiency of the furnace. Every furnace sold in America today has a label showing its Annual Fuel Utilization Efficiency (AFUE) Rating. This rating reflects the efficiency of a gas furnace in converting fuel to energy. A rating of 90 means that approximately 90% of the fuel is utilized to provide warmth to your home, while the remaining 10% escapes as exhaust.

The average furnace of 20 years ago was only 55 or 65% efficient. The government mandated that all furnaces had to have an AFUE of at least 78% efficient. Most moderately priced furnaces have AFUE's 80%. Furnaces with AFUE'S of 90 or better are considered high efficiency furnaces.

The furnaces with the highest efficiency rating also have the higher price point. If you are looking for the greatest economy, you have to determine how long it will take the furnace to pay you back the price differential in fuel savings.

40   New furnace technologies can make your home quieter, more comfortable and save you money

I have maintained for years that not every house was built for a 90 percent efficient (90 Plus) furnace. Older homes are not built tight enough and are usually not well enough insulated to take full advantage of a 90 Plus furnace, so it often didn't make sense to pay the extra money.

Many good HVAC contractors disagree with me about this and tell me that the opposite is true and that payback is actually quicker in an older house.

Some older people were also bothered by the longer, more powerful running cycle of 90 Plus furnaces, so I would often recommend that they not buy more than an 80 Plus furnace.

All this has changed with the introduction of the variable speed, 90 Plus furnaces such as the Lennox Signature G 61 Variable Speed, the Trane Two Stage Variable Speed, the Rheem Classic 90 Plus Modulating, the Ruud Achiever and the American Standard Variable Speed Two Stage Freedom 90. These furnaces have variable speed blower motors, some even have variable burn cycles which make them the most efficient, best operating, most economical, most comfortable furnaces on the market today. Also add that they are the best for your health.

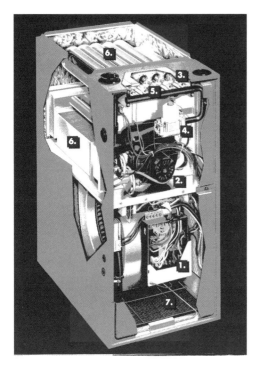

*Ultra high tech features
of the new breed of super
high efficiency furnaces
as illustrated by the Ruud
Achiever 90 Plus Gas
Furnace.*
1 Integrated furnace control
2 Draft inducer
*3 Direct spark ignition and
   remote sensor*
4 Gas valve and mainfold
5 In-shot burners
*6 Primary and secondary
   heat exchanger*

*Illustration courtesy of
Ruud Air Conditioning
Division (c) 2002*

Those are a lot of superlatives but I'll explain every one of them.

Most efficient:

These furnaces are rated in the mid to upper 90s for fuel efficiency. This means that almost none of your heating dollar is wasted. You get the full benefit of the natural gas you are burning.

The best of the 90 Plus, variable speed motors also have a variable manifold. If it is not very cold out and the furnace doesn't need to light the entire burner to heat the house efficiently, it doesn't. Using a smaller burner setting means the burner runs longer, heats the air more evenly, and runs more efficiently.

Best operating:

The most difficult things for any motor to do are start and stop. The new variable speed furnaces can be set to be running continuously. This greatly cuts down wear and tear on the blower motor.

Most economical:

The average furnace burns natural gas quite efficiently, but that is only half the equation. That same furnace also uses electric energy to run the blower motor. These electric motors are quite inefficient and prone to burn out at awkward times. They are one of the prime reasons your furnace stops in the middle of the night. The furnace is fine but the electric blower motor burned out so the furnace can't process the heat properly and has to shut down.

The new, variable speed 90 Plus furnaces have an entirely different type of electric motor that is so efficient it costs no more to run continuously than a 75 Watt light bulb. With this furnace you could save $250 to $300 on your electric bill every heating season. (The increased energy costs now coming into play could increase this figure greatly.) The motor also runs cooler and more efficiently so it should not need to be replaced as often, if ever.

Most comfortable:

The most irritating things furnaces do is start and stop. The average furnace burns a great deal of fuel fast, then the thermostat tells it to shut down, and on the average 90 percent efficient furnace, the blower motor keeps running until all the heated air is out of the duct work.

By the time the blower motor cycle is over it is blowing noticeably cooler air. For many people this is uncomfortable. When the furnace starts a little while later, the duct work is full of cool air and many people can feel an irritating breeze. Variable speed motors ramp up and down very slowly lessening the impact of this phenomenon.

By the way, most heating professionals tell me that this is untrue. I base my statements on the hundreds of reports I get from folks who are irritated by the cool drafts which the professionals say are not there.

No problem. The new 90 Plus variable speed furnaces can eliminate the problem by running continuously. The air in the ductwork never gets cold and there is a continuous warm air exchange throughout the house. That's comfort.

Best for your health:
In addition to heating the house, your furnace in cooperation with the humidifier and air filter, humidifies and filters the air. No matter how efficient the humidifier or filter is they can do nothing when the blower motor stops.

On their lowest setting the new variable speed furnaces can run continuously filtering air on a 24-hour per day basis. The air you breathe is therefore a good deal cleaner.

If you use a forced air, gas furnace, the high efficiency 90 Plus Variable Speed furnaces are way ahead of the rest of the pack. They are definitely extra quality, code plus, equipment.

Naturally their initial cost is higher than ordinary furnaces but they will recoup the extra cost in energy savings in just a few years and you will be rewarded by the extra quality for the life of the furnace.

That said, remember, the best furnace in the world is only as good as the contractor that installs it. All HVAC contractors are not equal. Do your homework.

Call the manufacturer and see if the company that wants to sell you a furnace is a certified installer. Are their technicians factory trained? How long have they been dealers?

Get and check references. You want to speak to people who had their furnace installed last year, two to three years ago, five years ago.

41 Natural gas forced air furnace is not always the best way to heat your house

Natural gas, forced air systems are the predominant type of heating installation in the US because of their relatively low installation cost and fuel availability. That is not true everywhere and the price of natural gas is escalating rapidly. Oil fired furnaces predominate in some parts of the United States.

Hydronic and boiler systems
Boiler systems such as those made by the Lennox Complete Heat and the American Water Heater Company use super efficient water heaters (boilers) to create highly efficient heating systems that also give almost unlimited supplies of hot water.

If you like to use your indoor hot tub a lot or have a large family that take lots of showers, the super water heating capacity alone make these systems very attractive.

Heat from the water heater can be used to heat air, which is then distributed through a forced air system, or the water heaters or boilers can be connected to a hydronic in-floor heating system.

Many people consider hydronic heat the most comfortable heating system. It is very popular in upscale homes because it keeps the floors warm and gives very even heat. If you want, you can also extend the hot water lines under exterior concrete to keep your driveway and sidewalks snow and ice free all winter long.

Geothermal systems

Geothermal is an excellent alternative and should save you money big time over the years. If you are presently using propane to heat your home, your fuel bill should be about one-fourth by converting to geothermal. That's very good. The installation cost of the system will probably be three or four times what you expect. That's not so good.

Up to four times more efficient than propane, a geothermal system doesn't really create heat. It shifts heat from the ground to your house in winter and from your house to the ground in summer. The heart of the geothermal system is the earth loop. Loops of high strength plastic pipe are buried either horizontally or vertically in the ground, lake or pond. A heat pump is used to direct heat from, or to, the ground.

To learn more, call a manufacturer of geothermal furnaces like The Water Furnace Co. The Geothermal Heat Pump Consortium has a very informative web site at www.geoexchange.org. The site includes information on geothermal systems, they call this type of heating "geoexchange". The site also lists manufacturers, local installers and the 20 states with incentive programs.

Be sure to tell your geothermal contractor that you want the option that provides continuous hot water. That will give free hot water as a side benefit.

Geothermal requires a constant source of electrical power to run the pumps that make the system work. Electric power can easily go out during a storm. If you decide to convert to geothermal, you should also install an electric generator that will come on automatically in the event of a power failure. Unfortunately, that generator will probably have to be powered by propane, but you shouldn't have to use it often.

42 Having the right humidity is the key to heating comfort

The old saying "It isn't the heat it's the humidity" is right. Dry air feels cooler than it really is. Warm air feels warmer than it really is.

If you keep turning up the thermostat during the winter and the house still feels cool, there is a good chance that your home has insufficient humidity.

Apparent Temperature for Values of Room Temperature and Relative Humidity

Relative Humidity (%)

Room temperature (°F)	0	10	20	30	40	50	60	70	80	90	100
75	68	69	71	72	74	75	76	76	77	78	79
74	66	68	69	71	72	73	74	75	76	77	78
73	65	67	68	70	71	72	73	74	75	76	77
72	64	65	67	68	70	71	72	73	74	75	76
71	63	64	66	67	68	70	71	72	73	74	75
70	63	64	65	66	67	68	69	70	71	72	73
69	62	63	64	65	66	67	68	69	70	71	72
68	61	62	63	64	65	66	67	68	69	70	71
67	60	61	62	63	64	65	66	67	68	68	69
66	59	60	61	62	63	64	65	66	67	67	68
65	59	60	61	61	62	63	64	65	65	66	67
64	58	59	60	60	61	62	63	64	64	65	66
63	57	58	59	59	60	61	62	62	63	64	64
62	56	57	58	58	59	60	61	61	62	63	63
61	56	57	57	58	59	59	60	60	61	61	62
60	55	56	56	57	58	58	59	59	60	60	61

Source: National Oceanic and Atmospheric Administration, Environmental Data and Information Service and Climatic Center.

If you have the heat set at 70 degrees but there is only 10% humidity, it will only feel like it is 65 degrees. If your true comfort level is 70 degrees, you will have to set the thermostat at over 75 degrees to be comfortable.

The easiest way to check this out is to buy an inexpensive hygrometer at the hardware store and check the humidity in various rooms throughout the house. The kitchen and bath may be fine but you will be surprised at how low the humidity gets in the living room and bedroom.

The humidity inside your house also has a relationship to the air outside. As the temperature decreases, the air's ability to hold water decreases and the relative humidity inside the house decreases.

Recommended indoor humidity levels

Outdoor Temperature Fahrenheit	Indoor Humidity
+40	45%
+30	40%
+20	35%
+10	30%
0	25%
-10	20%
-20	15%
Below -20	Move to Miami

The ideal humidity for human health and comfort is about 40%. It is good for our skin, nasal passages, eyes, you name it. It is also good for the plants and animals we choose to live with. The proper humidity also keeps wood, wool, plaster and many other construction materials in optimum condition.

When the cold outside air is brought into the house and heated, it becomes desert dry. Since dry air feels cooler than warm air, we often waste fuel by super heating our houses because the air does not contain sufficient humidity.

The easiest way to make certain the air has sufficient humidity is to have an efficient humidifier attached to the furnace. Different heating systems call for different types of humidification.

Natural Gas Forced Air

I believe that the most efficient humidifier for a forced air system is the flow-through, powered humidifier made by companies such as Bryant, Lennox, Skuttle, Research Products Aprilaire and Honeywell.

In flow-through humidifiers, a broad trickle of water flows over an evaporative pad. Unused water drains out of the system. The two biggest benefits of this type of humidifier are far greater efficiency than drum-style humidifiers and continuous flushing. Bryant's Deluxe Fan-Powered Humidifier delivers up to 25 gallons of moisture a day. Aprilaire's Model 760 A has an evaporative capacity of .75 gallons an hour or 18 gallons a day.

A minor drawback of the flow-through humidifier is that a small amount of water is wasted every year through drainage. I gladly pay this slight premium for increased health and comfort.

Other than Forced Air Furnaces

People who did not have forced air heat had to settle for portable humidifiers for many years. This is no longer the case.

There are now two types of humidifiers available for hydronic, baseboard and all other types of heating systems. The first type uses hot water and includes Research Products' Aprilaire 350 and 360. These humidifiers are either mounted under the floor or in the wall. Humidity is provided through a wall duct.

The second type of humidifier includes high-capacity, steam-powered models such as the Skuttle 60 and the Honeywell HE 420/460. They are often used with heat pumps and Space Pak high-velocity forced air systems. Since the humidification is created through internally produced steam, they can add humidity even at 70 degrees F.

43   A top quality programmable thermostat is the key to the best use of your home's heating and cooling equipment

A programmable thermostat can save you 10% or 20% on heating and cooling bills. The government estimates you can save 10% by simply turning the thermostat back 10% to 15% for 8-hours during a 24-hour period.

That means that during the heating season, if you turn the heat down when you go to bed at night or leave for work, you save 10%. If you remember to turn it down at both times, you could double the savings.

If you reverse the process during the cooling season and turn the thermostat up when you go to bed at night, and up when you leave for work during the day, you would get similar savings on your cooling bills.

One of the easiest ways to make sure the temperature is turned up and down at the proper times is to install and use a programmable thermostat.

 Most programmable thermostats will let you set 4 to 6 different temperature settings during a 24-hour period. You can also have different weekday and weekend settings. Some will let you program each day separately.

Thermostats like the Honeywell 8600 or the Bryant Thermo Distat, can be equipped with outside sensors and control heating, cooling and humidification to provide a total comfort system.

The top of the line Lennox programmable thermostat has a feature that will even dehumidify air if the temperature setting is already met. It does this by automatically increasing the setting by two degrees if it senses that there is too much humidity in the air.

44 Not all air conditioners are created equal

The best air conditioner is the one that is sized right and installed correctly

There are only about 8 major manufacturers of air conditioning equipment and hundreds, maybe thousands, of different brand names. Since so much of the equipment is similar the installing contractor's reputation for prompt, dependable service and expertise is far more important than brand name.

Contractor's reputations being equal you would judge the central air conditioning unit on operating efficiency, refrigerant, size, noise level, product design, and warranty.

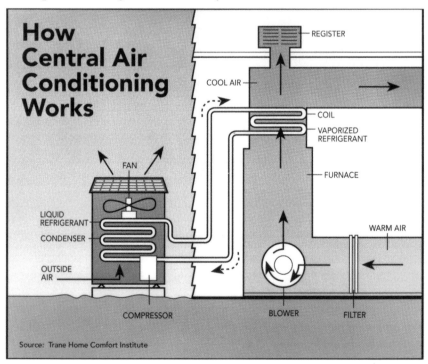

How Central Air Conditioning Works

Source: Trane Home Comfort Institute

No matter what the brand or the efficiency rating on the label, the best air conditioner is the one that is sized correctly. An air conditioner is designed to "condition" air. That means that it removes moisture and cools the air before the furnace blower motor distributes it throughout the house.

If the compressor is undersized, it may not be able to do the job. If it is oversized, it will chill the air too fast and the air will have been cooled but not dehumidified. This will result in a cold, dank feeling house.

Heat Load Study critical

Before a contractor can make an intelligent quote on your air conditioning, he should perform a Heat Load Study. Among other things, the Heat Load Study considers the size of your house, the amount of roof and wall insulation, number and size of windows, as well as the direction they face, the color of the roof, your cooling requirements by time of day, and the number and type of trees giving shade and/or providing wind blocks.

You should also tell the contractor how cool you want the house on a 95-degree Fahrenheit afternoon; where the hottest rooms in the house are located; whether it is important to have the upstairs bedrooms cool in the afternoon or if they just have to be cool in the evening.

When all this information is turned into numerical values, a simple calculation gives the contractor the information he needs to properly size your home's air conditioning.

Don't do business with a lazy contractor

Many contractors do not want to do all this work and will try to base their air conditioning quotes on your old air conditioner. This is not a good idea because most new air conditioners are 47% more efficient than those made 20-years ago.

Your house today, is probably not the same house you had 20 years ago either. You may well have added insulation, upgraded windows, re-roofed, or had trees planted or removed. Each of these factors can make a big difference in the size of the air conditioning unit you require.

Let's go shopping
A central air conditioning system consists of an indoor and an outdoor unit. The outdoor unit is a metal box called the condenser that includes a condensing coil, a compressor and a fan.

The most important feature of the indoor unit is the evaporator coil, which is usually located inside the furnace or air handler. The furnace blows hot air from inside the home through the evaporator coil, cooling the air. The cooled air is then routed throughout the home, via the air ducts.

As the inside air is chilled, the refrigerant inside the evaporator coil is heated. The heated refrigerant is cycled to the outdoor unit where it is compressed and cooled, then recycled indoors to cool more hot air.

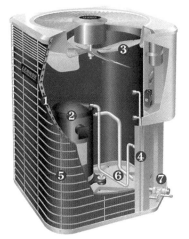

One of the most common mistakes is for the air conditioning contractor to specify a compressor too large for the house. When this happens the compressor runs for too short a period of time and the air does not get dehumidified.
An over-sized air conditioner also turns on and off far more frequently. Turning on and off is very hard on an air conditioner and dramatically increases wear.

This cut away illustration of a Lennox Elite HSX12 air conditioner shows some of the key elements you will find in a top of the line unit. 1- high-efficiency outdoor coil, 2- scroll type compressor, 3- direct drive fan, 4- corrosion-resistant cabinet, 5- enhanced coil guard, 6- drainage holes and 7- high-pressure safety switch.   Illustration courtesy of Lennox Industries (c) 2002

Things to look for when choosing an air conditioner

Most systems are pretty much the same but three improvements have been made in some units in recent years.

Scroll type compressors

The majority of air conditioners use noisy piston-type compressors. One of the air conditioning industry's major suppliers, the Copeland Co., has developed a revolutionary scroll technology that is quieter, more efficient and longer-lived than piston compressors. Scroll compressors are now included in most air conditioning manufacturers' top-of-the-line units.

Two-speed motors

Air conditioners can have one or two speeds. Single-speed motors create a draft that pushes cold air through the ductwork at a high rate of speed. Two-stage air conditioners use a lower speed the majority of the time to create a more comfortable airflow, cut the fluctuation in room temperature and reduce humidity. Two speed motors are worth the extra money.

Stealth technology

Lennox has incorporated the same "stealth" propeller design elements into their compressor fan that is used on the propellers powering our submarine fleet. Combining this very quiet fan with greatly increased sound conditioning makes the Lennox compressor so quiet that it would take 20 Lennox condensing units running side by side to equal the noise level of the loudest comparable competitive condensing unit.

Seasonal Energy Efficiency Rating

Air conditioning and heat pump equipment are now given a Seasonal Energy Efficiency Rating (SEER) by the Air-Conditioning Rating Institute. The SEER rating projects the unit's operating efficiency over an entire cooling season. The lowest rated central air conditioner allowed by the government is 10 SEER. By 2006, the threshold will increase to 12 SEER. Every time you increase the SEER rating you decrease the amount of energy used but increase the price of the unit.

The US Department of Energy says that you can save enough on energy costs to cover the increased price of a 12 SEER rated air conditioner in just a few years. Their pay back estimate is based on a seasonal average of 1,500 cooling hours.

To give the devil their due skyrocketing energy costs may reduce payback times greatly. However, using the governments numbers, if you live in Michigan, New York, Illinois and most northern tier states, you only average 600 cooling hours a year, not 1,500 hours. Your pay back period on a 12 SEER air conditioner is 2.5 times longer than the national average.

On the other hand, the hotter the temperature and the greater the number of cooling hours you have, the more you save with an air conditioner that has a high SEER rating.

If you live in the southern tip of Florida, you would average 2,800 cooling hours. It would only take about half the national average time to start saving with a more efficient air conditioner.

Lennox and Trane make super high efficiency air conditioning units rated at over 19 SEER. If you live in Michigan, buying one of these super high efficiency units would be ridiculous. However, if you live in Texas or South Florida, they could save you buckets of money.

New coolants are a mixed blessing
Most air conditioners use a refrigerant called R-22. This refrigerant will not be manufactured after 2020. A new refrigerant called R-410 A will take its place. Current trade names of R-410 A are Puron by Bryant, Prozone by Ruud, Environ by Lennox and Genetron AZ-20 by Allied Signal Inc.

R-410 A is more environmentally friendly than R-22 but not all air conditioning experts are happy with the new refrigerant.

On the pro side, the new refrigerant has no chlorine, which is better for the atmosphere. On the good/bad side, the operating pressure of an R-410 A compressor is 50 percent higher than conventional models. This requires compressor wall thickness, which results in a quieter compressor.

On the con side, an R-410 A system is more susceptible to moisture damage.

Consider replacing the air conditioner and furnace at the same time

Although the air conditioner cools and dehumidifies the air it is up to the power of the furnace blower motor to distribute it. The heated air the blower motor distributes in the winter is light and relatively easy to move. Hot air rises naturally.

Cold air is heavy and wants to sink. In many houses the blower motor has to literally push the air up and out of the basement into the rest of the house. Getting the air to the first floor is hard, getting it to the second floor much harder.

If you have an old furnace with a blower motor that is on its last legs, it may be totally inadequate during the cooling season. In that case it would make good sense to take the systems approach and replace the furnace and the air conditioner at the same time. That way you can buy the companion furnace designed by the manufacturer to meet the exact demand requirements of your new air conditioner.

45   Pay attention to the air you breathe and you may breathe a lot longer

Since you only have one set of lungs it makes good sense to be as nice to them as possible. Most of us spend 60 to 90 percent of our time indoors. Indoor air can be anywhere from 2 to 70 times more polluted than outside air.

At home and at work we wade through an invisible sea of up to 20 to 30 million microscopic particles per cubic meter of air. Every day, each of us breathes about 20,000 times. During that time, each of us inhales about 200 million invisible respiratory particles.

All of these particles create a tremendous strain on our bronchial systems and can have a devastating effect on our health. Approximately 65 million of us suffer from allergies, asthma and other respiratory problems.

According to the American College of Allergists, one-half of all illnesses are either caused or aggravated by poor indoor air quality. The average person spends about $700 per year for asthma or sinusitis treatment and $311 for allergy treatment. The Environmental Protection Agency ranks poor indoor air quality as one of the top five environmental risks.

Government regulations provide minimum criteria for workplace air quality. We have the responsibility of maintaining the air quality in our homes. The better job we do, the better we and our families feel and the less time and money we spend in doctor's offices and drug stores.

Improving the air quality in our homes with an effective air purification system can drastically cut down the number of particulates in the house and make our homes a healthier place in which to live.

A good filter is a good way to clean the air

The furnace filter is very important to both you and your furnace. Unfortunately, the fiberglass filter used in most furnaces is just designed to protect the furnace from dust balls and to provide hunks and chunks that might damage the equipment. It does nothing to improve the quality of the air inside the house.

To actually make your home's air quality better the filter has to be greatly improved.

Filters and air cleaners screen out particles suspended in the air. The standard unit of measurement for these particulates is the micron. A micron is one millionth of a meter or 1/25,400 of an inch.

To give you an indication how small that is, the dot above this letter "i" is 397 microns. The eye of the average needle is 749 microns wide and a one-inch square postage stamp measures 25,400 microns per side. As a general rule, anything below 40 microns in size is invisible to the human eye.

Airborne particulates range from specks 100 microns down to less than 0.01 microns. Only 2% of all pollutants measure between 100 and 2 microns in size. 98% of all pollutants measure between just fewer than 2 microns and 0.01 microns.

Aqua-Air Technologies, Inc., the makers of EnviroSept very high efficiency electronic air filters, has two excellent charts on air borne particle sizes and "hang times" on their web site.

They divide the 20 million particles found in an average air sampling into size categories then explain how long the various sizes tend to hang in the air. The smaller the particulate, the longer it stays airborne, the more apt we are to breathe it into our lungs.

Micron Size Range	Proportionate Quantity
Over 10	1,000
Between 5 – 10	35,000
Between 3 – 5	50,000
Between 1 & 3	214,000
Between .5 and 1	1,352,000
Between .01 and .05	18,280,000

Particle hang time, they call it Settling Rate is just as eye opening. The larger the particle, the sooner it settles. A 10-micron particle will only hang for 5 minutes. But a 5-micron particle will hang for 20-minutes. A 1-micron particle will hang for 6-1/2 hours. Particles less than 1 micron in size are considered "permanently suspended".

The American Lung Association says that pollutants measuring 4 microns and below are the most dangerous to our health. Particles smaller than 2.5 microns are called "respirable" because they are breathed deep into the lungs every time we inhale.

Amaircare, the makers of Air Wash HEPA whole house air filtration systems, created the following chart to illustrate the relative sizes of various pollutants.

The sizes shown are in microns. As I said before, one micron equals one millionth of a meter.

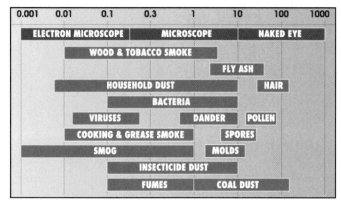

Chart courtesy of Amaircare Corporation

When you combine this information, you find that the smaller the particle, the more dangerous it is and the longer it will stay in the air. If you don't want those particles in your air, you have to filter them out.

There is now a widely accepted, independently tested national standard so that you can compare apples to apples when you are filter shopping or thinking about upgrading your heating and cooling systems air cleaning capacity.

The test was developed by the American Society of Heating, Refrigeration & Air Conditioning Engineers (ASHRAE). The new testing procedure is covered in ASHRAE 52.2-1999. It is a big step up because it calls for a series of tests that use chemically generated potassium chloride (KCl) Dust to determine Minimum Efficiency Reporting Value (MERV) for the filter being tested. The KCl dust range from 0.3 to 10 microns in size.

Because the MERV rating denotes the MINIMUM efficiency of the filter rated, you can depend upon the number not being advertising agency bombast. That is a definite plus.

If you want to learn a great deal more about MERV ratings, Dr. W. J. Kowalski in conjunction with Dr. W. P. Bahnfleth of Penn State have written an excellent monograph on MERV Filter Ratings, entitled MERV Filter Models for Aerobiological Applications. It is available on the web at www.arche.psu.edu/iec/abe/MERVAM.html.

The Association of the Nonwoven Fabrics Industry is an organization of manufacturers that make everything from the fabrics used in filters to roofing and baby diapers. On their web site the inda defines and ranks furnace filters in the following order (low to high):

Traditional Fiberglass or Polyester: "inexpensive, disposable, 1" filters recommended to be changed monthly…not very effective at capturing smaller, respirable particles from the air."

Washable/Reusable: "1" filters…designed to be washed out monthly and reused. While…initially expensive, it can be used for a number of years….Tests show that this type of filter is not very effective at capturing smaller respirable particles from the air….some brands of this filter claim an electrostatic charge…(but) the charge is actually minimal and plays little or no role in particle capture."

Ordinary Flat or Pleated: "It is recommended that these disposable, 1" filters be changed every 2 or 3 months. These filters are generally made out of a cotton or polyester media that is denser than fiberglass and will typically capture more small particles. The filters can be found with either a pleated or flat media."

Deep Pleated: "Deep pleated filters are either 5" or 6" deep and thus can only be used on heating and cooling systems that are specially adapted to accept them….media needs to be replaced once or twice a year. These filters have been shown to demonstrate a broad range of efficiency levels between various brands. The efficiency of some brands is only slightly higher than that of fiberglass while others approach the performance of a permanently charged electrostatic filter."
(editor's note: All the furnace companies thick media filters are in this category)

Pleated, Permanently Charged Electrostatic: "These 1", disposable filters need to be changed only once every 2 to 3 months. Like the four previously mentioned…this type is also designed to physically capture particles. But its efficiency in trapping smaller, respirable particles is better than other 1" air filters and most of the deep pleated filters because its electret fibers are electrostatically charged. Particles which would otherwise have passed through, are: magnetically" drawn to the filter. This filter type represents an

alternative to the more costly electronic air cleaners for households trying to improve their indoor air quality."
(editor's note: 3M Filtrete filters are in this category.)

Electronic Air Cleaner: "This type of air filter is a permanent fixture in the heating and cooling system and requires an electrical connection. Although it is significantly more expensive than any other type of air filter, it is very effective at removing particles from the air. However it must be disassembled and cleaned regularly to keep its high level of effectiveness. Also, these air cleaners may emit ozone, which can be harmful."

HEPA: Although not listed on the inda web site the HEPA (High Efficiency Particulate Arrestance) filter is rapidly growing in popularity. Whole house HEPA filters represent one of the highest forms of air filtration available today.

As filters grow more effective, they offer more and more resistance to the furnace blower motor. Because of their ultra high efficiency, whole house HEPA filters are called "Stand Alone Bypass Filters". They have their own power supply and blower system and act independently from the furnace. The furnace therefore needs an additional filter to protect the blower motor.

Inda gives the following MERV estimates for the various types of filters.
    Flat Throwaway: 0 to 1 MERV
    Pleated Throwaway: 3 to 6 MERV
    Deep Pleated: 8 to 10 MERV
    Electrostatic Pleated: 8 to 12 MERV

HEPA filters: 16 to 20 MERV As (per Ron Wlkinson, P.E., for MC2 Market & Competitive Convergence, www.mc2link.com.

Both the 3M Filtrete Ultra Allergen Filter and the AllergyZone filter have earned ratings of MERV 12. They both cost in the $20 to $25 range and should be replaced every three months.

Electronic air cleaners are often sold as a furnace filter upgrade. They are far more expensive initially and can be extremely efficient when new. However they take a great deal of maintenance and very few homeowners take care of them properly. Since a dirty electronic air cleaner ceases to be effective many (perhaps most) people who buy electronic air cleaners but fail to live up to the rigid maintenance schedules receive little or no benefit.

Environmental Dynamics Group and Aqua-Air Technologies, Inc. make electronic air cleaners, which combine the disposability of a media filter with the efficiency of an electronic air cleaner. These units cost less than standard electronic air cleaners and may well do a better cleaning job because the dirty media collector pads are thrown away.

If you forget and let the filter get extremely dirty, filter power is not diminished. Filter pads last for about 3 months.

If you want to maximize air filtration further, it is necessary to upgrade to a "stand alone" HEPA filter unit that works in conjunction with the furnace but is separated from it and does not put any strain on the furnace blower system.

Two commonly available HEPA systems are the Amaircare Air Wash and the Broan-Nutone Guardian Plus.

The Amaircare Air Wash is a 100 percent sealed system and uses a pre-filter, HEPA filter and carbon filter to do an extremely efficient air cleaning job. The unit runs continuously and constantly sends a stream of filtered air throughout the house. It is also connected to a Skuttle model 216 and, whenever it senses negative air pressure, brings in a supply of fresh outdoor air to freshen the indoor air. It is available from Lennox dealers in the US.

The Broan-Nutone Guardian Plus combines both a HEPA air filter and a Heat Recovery Ventilator in one system. This combines air filtration, air makeup and heat recovery into a very cost efficient package.

46 Ultra Violet light can increase air quality

Ultraviolet light is the newest weapon in the battle against bad air. The greatest source of UV is the sun. Its rays bleach furniture and fabrics and turn wooden decks gray. We use sunscreens, sunglasses and hats to protect our skin and eyes from its power. If we let our skin go unprotected from UV rays for an extended period of time they can cause serious injury including cancer.

UV waves are even more dangerous to bacteria, molds, mold spores and viruses. They penetrate cell walls and change the organisms' DNA, making cell reproduction impossible.

Technology using UV has been available commercially for 40 years but germicidal quality UV equipment, technically UV germicidal irradiation (UVGI), has only been introduced on the residential level recently.

Not all UV lights are created equal. Some create ozone. Some do not. Ozone is an unstable O3 molecule. Some systems use relatively small, very powerful UV lights, some use larger, lower power lights.

Penn State University is currently in the process of creating a UV rating system similar to the MERV rating system for filters. It is called the UVGI (Ultra Violet Germicidal Irradiation) Rating Value or URV. Once the rating system has become widely accepted it will make comparing UV germicidal systems a great deal easier.

Typically, UV lights are placed in three places: in the supply air plenum to disinfect molds and spores on the air conditioning coils; in the return air plenum to disinfect return air; and, most recently, in direct connection to a thick or pleated media filter.

Currently Honeywell has a one UV light/thick media filter system and Lennox has both a 4 UV light/ pleated media system called the PCO-12C for average-sized houses with heating systems up to 3 tons and a 6 UV/ pleated media system called the PCO-20C for larger houses with heating systems of up to 5 tons called the PureAir Air Purification system.

Lennox Pure Air Plus PCO-20C with pre-filter, 6 UV lights, titanium dioxide-coated metal mesh and thick media filter.

During a 24-hour period, Jim Williams of Williams Refrigeration and Heating, reports that the Lennox PureAir Air Purification system removes 75 percent of all airborne particulates, 60 percent of all bioaerosols and destroys 50 percent of all odors and airborne chemicals.

Dr. W. J. Kowalski of Penn State University and Charles E. Dunn, Sr., President and CEO of Lumalier, a state of the art UV germicidal lighting developer and manufacturer, wrote a monograph entitled "Current Trends in UVGI Air and Surface Disinfection.

In the paper they speculate that air cleaning which combined a UVGI light with a MERV 6 air filter would even be an excellent defense in the event of terrorist attack. It could even be effective against Anthrax and Smallpox spores and TB Bacilli.

If you have access to the web, you will find Kowalski and Dunn's paper on the Lumalier web site, www.lumalier.com/E/H2.htm.

For more information on the use of UV lights in conjunction with your heating and cooling system consult:

* AirPal: www.airpalspectra.com
* Airtech International Group Inc.: www.airtechgroup.com
* Field Controls: www.fieldcontrols.com
* Nirvana Safe Haven: www.nontoxic.com/air/index.html
* Second Wind: www.freshpureair.com
* Honeywell: www.honeywell.com/yourhome/uvelite/uv100a.htm
*Lennox: www.lennox.com
* Commercial Lighting Design, Inc. Lumalier, (800) 774-5799, www.lumalier.com

47 The best way to maximize air quality is to use a combined system approach

The ultimate air cleaning system at the time of printing is a stand alone HEPA bypass filter such as the Amaircare AirWash System used in conjunction with a UV light/media filter and a modulating, variable speed furnace.

The variable speed furnace allows the blower motor to run continuously assuring constant air cleaning by the UV light/media filter. This combines with the independently powered HEPA bypass filter to assure that the air is cleaned and sanitized 24-hours a day.

The Amaircare HEPA filters and AirWash system are distributed by Indoor Air Quality Distributors. Both the Amaircare AirWash and the Lennox UV/Media Filter combination are available from Lennox dealers.

48   Air make up units solve negative air pressure problems

The average house of today is built much tighter than the house of 50 to 100 years ago. At the same time our furnaces, dryer vents and assorted kitchen and bath fans continuously suck heat out of the house.

In these circumstances it is very easy for the house to "go negative". That means more air is being forced out of the house than is able to come into the house. This creates a partial vacuum.

All sorts of bad things can happen when a house goes negative. Not enough fresh air comes into the house so the indoor air becomes dank, stagnant and unhealthy. Cooking and other odors linger. During the winter, drafts are common and water condenses on windows. Fireplaces back draft either filling the room with smoke or spreading a smell of wet ashes days after the fire. Annoying "Zebra stripes" can appear on outside walls and ceilings and you can't get rid of them no matter what you do.

The only way to stop these things from happening is to balance the air pressure in the house. This is best done by installing air makeup devices such as the Xavier Equaliz-Air or the Skuttle Model 216. Both units allow fresh air to be drawn into the house when needed to equalize air pressure.

The Skuttle is connected to the ductwork and works through the furnace. The Equaliz-Air unit functions independently of the furnace and is actually more sensitive than the Skuttle and other similar units.

Skuttle Model 216.
Photo courtesy of Skuttle Corp.

HRV (Heat Recovery Ventilators) and ERV(Energy Recover Ventilators) like the Honeywell units pictured here conserve heat while equalizing air pressure loss caused by the operation of the furnace.

Photo courtesy of Honeywell Inc.

The Amaircare stand alone HEPA By Pass Filter brings in fresh aire and equalizes air pressure. The Broan-Nutone Guardian Plus combines air make up and a Heat Recovery Ventilator with a HEPA air filter in one system. This is a very efficient way to solve the negative air problem, save energy through heat recovery and add the benefit of HEPA air filtration.

49 The roof, insulation and attic venting create a cold roof system that protects your home

If you ask the average person, you will learn that shingles protect the house from rain and snow. Insulation saves energy by stopping heat loss during the winter and keeping the home cooler during the summer. Attic ventilation does something or other, who knows what, to protect the shingles.

All this is true enough but to learn what these elements really do you have to understand that the attic is supposed to be totally divorced from the rest of the house and have its own independent atmosphere. This is called the "Cold Roof Theory."

Under this theory attic insulation and ventilation are used to keep the underside of the roof deck cold. Keeping the underside of the deck cool provides optimum conditions for the longevity of the shingles and roof decking. It should also eliminate ice damming.

This Owens Corning illustration of attic and roofing components work together to protect the house. They include the attic insulation, soffit vent, rafter baffle channeling soffit vent air to ridge, waterproof underlayment at drip edge, valleys and vents, chimney and skylight (not shown), shingles and ridge vent. Illustration courtesy of Owens Corning © 2000

If the entire system is installed properly and works well, the roof and shingles last for many years and the insulation saves the homeowner money on heating and cooling costs.

Installed improperly and working inefficiently and the shingles curl and degrade, the roof deck rots, roof dams form on the shingles making water damage probable, the insulation gets soggy or brittle from condensation and the attic has a high potential for developing black mold.

To compound the problem many marginal roofers and insulation installers do not know and do not want to take the time and effort to learn how the work they do integrates to create the cold roof system.

Many roofers and insulation contractors do not want to "waste" their time building proper ventilation into the attic even though proper ventilation is the vital ingredient that allows roofing and insulation to do their jobs.

Although attic insulation saves money on heating and cooling costs its most vital function is to isolate the attic from the rest of the house. The purpose of soffit and ridge vent ventilation is to cool the underside of the roof deck and keep the attic temperature as close as possible to the outside temperature.

If your house is build in accordance with the cold roof theory, it is vital that the entire roof/insulation/attic venting system be in place and operating effectively if your house is to be safe.

50 Your roofline says a lot about you

If you live in a single-story house or a multi-level house, one of the first things a person sees when they drive up to your house is the roof. When it comes time to sell, the attractiveness of the roofline can be the difference between perspective buyers driving by or getting out of the car and taking a look at the house.

All other aspects aside this makes the roofing on your home very important.

More than just being a "pretty face" however, your roof is also your homes first light of defense against the elements.

Organic and fiberglass shingles are almost the same
The vast majority of residential roofs are covered with fiberglass or organic shingles. Both fiberglass and organic shingles are classified as asphalt. The only difference between the two shingles is the mat upon which the shingle is made. If the mat is felt paper, the shingle is called organic. If the mat is made out of fiberglass, the shingle is called fiberglass.

The rest of the shingle is composed of one or more layers of asphalt and granules and adhesive. Granules give the shingle its reflective quality, color and UV (ultra violet) ray protection. Asphalt holds the granules and provides a tough watertight seal. Adhesive helps the shingle lay flat and withstand the winds.

Organic shingles are slightly heavier than fiberglass. If you are in a high wind area or the extreme North, organic has the edge. If you are in a high fire risk area or where it is very hot, fiberglass has the edge.

Multi-layer gives maximum curb appeal

One-layer shingles are called single ply. Two and three layer shingles are the high end of the asphalt shingle market and are called laminates or multi-layer shingles. The lamination provides the shingle with a layered color effect and an increased shadow line- to give a three-dimensional look. This depth and color is easily discernible from ground level and greatly increases the curb appeal of the house.

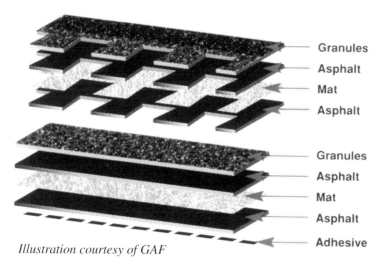

Granules
Asphalt
Mat
Asphalt

Granules
Asphalt
Mat
Asphalt
Adhesive

Illustration courtesy of GAF

The extra thickness also adds extra strength and weight. A single ply shingle often weighs around 225 pounds per square of 100 square feet. A two ply shingle weighs over 300 pounds and a premium 3-ply shingle will often weigh 400 to 425 pounds.

Owens Corning says high-end laminated shingles are now 35 percent of the market.

If you don't know whether multi-layer shingles are worth the added price, take a drive around your neighborhood. If all the new roofs have single-ply shingles, you can have single-ply also. If quite a few homes have attractive shadow lines, investing your money in laminated shingles is a good idea.

As the thickness of the shingle goes up, so does the price and the length of the warranty. Depending on the shingle, warranties can extend from 10 to 50 years. A few of the premium shingles even have a lifetime warranty.

Not all shingle manufacturers' warranties are alike. GAF has an elite installer program in which the entire job, both materials and workmanship, is inspected and guaranteed by the company. Certainteed has a similar program.

Workmanship is usually guaranteed by the installing contractor. No matter how good the installer, he could fall off a roof and go out of business at any moment. The GAF and Certainteed programs take the worry out of workmanship and are worth the extra money.

51 Insulation is the best home improvement you can buy

Insulation is like temperature armor. It works to protect the temperature inside your home from being affected by the outside temperature. During the summer it keeps your house cooler. During the winter it keeps your house warmer.

By doing this it saves tremendous amounts of money you would otherwise have to spend on heating and cooling. Dollar for dollar it usually gives you the biggest and most rapid return on your home improvement investment dollar.

A very important side benefit of attic insulation is that it keeps heat from rising into the attic and warming the underside of the roof deck boards. By doing this it makes the cold roof theory that I wrote about in Tip 48 possible.

Loose fill fiberglass or cellulose insulation can be sprayed on attic floors or in walls. Photo courtesy of Owens Corning

The amount of insulation your house needs depends upon where you live

The amount of insulation your house needs depends upon where it is located. The US Department of Energy (DOE) has insulation recommendations for attics, walls, floors, crawl space, concrete slabs and the interior and exterior of basement walls.

When we talk about insulation, we talk about the "R-value". R-value stands for heat flow resistance. The higher the R-value, the greater the insulation's ability to withstand the transfer of heat.

US Insulation Requirements

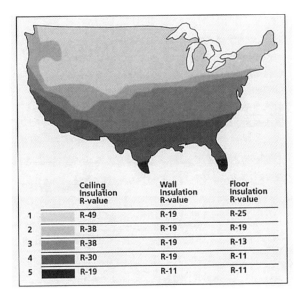

	Ceiling Insulation R-value	Wall Insulation R-value	Floor Insulation R-value
1	R-49	R-19	R-25
2	R-38	R-19	R-19
3	R-38	R-19	R-13
4	R-30	R-19	R-11
5	R-19	R-11	R-11

If you live anywhere other than California, Hawaii and the southern tips of Texas, Louisiana and Florida, the insulation on the floor of the attic should have a value of R-49, a cathedral ceiling needs R-38, and walls should have R-18. People with electric heat should increase attic insulation to R-60 in the coldest states.

As of this writing, the insulation recommendation for Ontario, Canada is R-31 for attics and R-17 for walls. This is not nearly enough and Canadians would do well to use US standards wherever the US recommendations are higher.

The Owens Corning web site has a very handy interactive page that will give you the exact US Department of Energy insulation recommendations for your zip code at om/around/insulation/rvalue.asp" *www.owenscorning.com/around/insulation/rvalue.asp*.

The Department of Energy also has an excellent Insulation fact sheet, DOE/CE-0180 2002, developed at Oak Ridge National

Laboratory. It will not only give you insulation recommendations based upon your zip code but a great deal of other insulation information as well. You will find the fact sheet on the web at *www.ornl.gov/roofs+walls/insulation/ins_16.html.*

The best way to find out how much insulation you need to add is to find out how much you already have

The amount of insulation you have depends upon the age of your house. Most of us have fiberglass insulation in the attic and little or no insulation in the walls. Older U.S. houses have R-9 or less. Many Canadian homes were built before they had insulation requirements.

To compute how much insulation your house has, go up to the attic with a ruler. If the insulation is 3 inches thick, the R-Value is roughly R-9. If it's 6 inches, R-19; 10 inches, R-30; and 13 inches, R-42.

If the insulation in your attic is at least a foot thick, you have sufficient insulation. If the insulation is only 3 to 6 inches thick, you need a great deal more. Tell the contractor that you want the attic insulation to be increased to R-49. That is about 15 inches of fiberglass. Cellulose insulation is a little denser, so you might only need a blanket of 12 or 13 inches to have the required thickness of insulation.

If you just have to add a layer of fiberglass insulation on the attic floor, you might want to do it yourself and could save some money. If your house is already constructed and you want to add insulation to the walls, you do not have the skill required to do the job.

If you have a major insulation job, I suggest you find out what all your costs will be, then get quotes from professional contractors. The cost is usually so close that it doesn't make sense not to let someone else do the work .

Insulation choices

The standard insulation materials for ceilings and walls are loose or batt fiberglass insulation and loose cellulose insulation. Icynene and other foams are more efficient but are also more costly. Rock wool or slag wool insulation is available but seldom used.

Fiberglass batts are the most popular way to add insulation to attics because they are easy to use and add a pre-determined R-value. For example, Owens Corning offers 6-1/4-inch-thick R-19 batts; 9-1/2-inch-thick R-30 batts, and special Miraflex 8-3/4-inch-thick R-25 batts. If you were starting from scratch and wanted to develop an R-49 insulation blanket, you could use one layer of 9-1/2 R-30 batt and one 6-1/4 R-19 batt.

Batts come faced or unfaced. Faced batts have craft paper on one side, which acts as a vapor barrier. Unfaced batts do not have the craft paper. Unfaced batts are recommended for attics. If you use faced batts in the attic, lay the batt paper side down.

Some batts also come in perforated poly wrap. This makes the batts easier to use and more expensive but does nothing to increase R-value or act as a vapor barrier.

Loose fiberglass and loose cellulose come in bags and can be sprayed on attic floors to the desired depth or sprayed into wall cavities. Both these products take a high level of skill on the part of the installer but give a superior job.

Other insulation choices include rock wool, spray foam and rigid foam insulation. Rock wool was used a great deal many years ago but is seldom used in residential insulation today.

Rigid and spray foams are usually used as special purpose insulation materials. Rigid foam is often used in basements and crawl spaces. Spray foams like Icynene can be used under roofs and in walls and wherever a very compact insulation material is required.

Cans of urethane foam, like Great Stuff, are used as spot insulation around electrical receptacles, around band joists and where ever pipes penetrate the building envelope.

52 The rest of the house also needs insulation

The Department of Energy Map shown earlier in this chapter showed the recommended insulation for attics, cathedral ceilings, walls, floors, crawl spaces, slab edges and basements.

Illustration courtesy of
Owns Corning

Many older homes have little or no insulation in the walls. The easiest way to add wall insulation to a pre-existing structure is to blow in loose cellulose or fiberglass from the outside.

The Do-It-Yourselfer can insulate around sill plates with foam or stuffed-in fiberglass. Anything below grade like basement walls are best insulated with rigid foam.

The one place you can add insulation under the floor is in uninsulated crawl spaces. The standard practice is to use rigid foam on the underside of crawl space walls and have air vents on at least two of the walls.

I have to tell you that there is a new theory being thrashed out concerning crawl spaces. The new theory is to make the crawl space into a totally sealed, insulated, void that allows no heat, cold or moisture to penetrate and be passed on to the house above it.

This sounds good and is technically feasible. The old way of treating crawlspaces often developed problems. I will keep watching the technical reviews and let you know if I recommend sealed crawl spaces in five or ten years.

One last word. Remember: cans of spray foam are one of the Do-It-Yourselfer's best friends. Even if you can't get to a void that should be plugged or insulated, your friend in the aerosol can get there with ease.

One word of caution, remember there are both expanding and non-expanding foams. Go wild with an expanding foam and you can do a lot of damage. When working in a delicate area, use a non-expanding foam.

Many home centers carry expanding foam in the gallon size. If you are doing a major project, get the gallon. It is less expensive to use and you will not run out nearly as often.

53 Attic ventilation and how it works

A good rule of thumb is that whenever you add insulation you should add ventilation. Attic insulation isolates the attic from the rest of the house.

Proper ventilation keeps a cooling upward draft flowing from the soffit to the ridge vent year round. Ideally this draft keeps the underside of the roof deck boards the same temperature as the ambient outside temperature.

The upward stream of air from soffit to ridge is called passive ventilation. All we have to do is provide the opening for it to happen and mother nature does all the work.

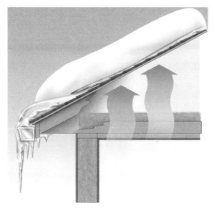

This excellent Owens Corning illustration shows how heat penetrates the attic through insufficient insulation and warms the underside of the deck boards. This warmth melts snow on top of the roof which forms ice dams on gutters.

Water from additional melting snow is blocked by the ice dams and backs up the roof. Eventually the water may get underneath some shingles and leak into the attic causing water damage.

Illustrations courtesy of Owens Corning

Under the cold roof theory, it is impossible to have too much venting in the attic. Continuous soffit vents and ridge venting would be ideal.

Air from the soffit vents should be directed upward with rafter baffles. Rafter baffles are pieces of rigid Styrofoam that are inserted between the rafters at the base of the roof and direct air up the roofline to the ridge vent. They also serve to keep the soffit vents from being blocked by insulation.

If it is inconvenient to have a continuous soffit vent for some reason, a soffit vent every other rafter should be sufficient.

If you cannot install ridge venting, pot vents should be installed as close to the top of the roof as possible. Pot vents that are installed below the top third of the roofline actually obstruct attic ventilation.

One pot vent is required for every 150 square feet of attic. To determine the number of pot vents required, multiply the length of the attic times the width, then divide by 150.

Many older homes have gable vents, which allow air to come in from the side of the house. This sideways rush of incoming air disrupts the upward flow of air from soffit to ridge and stops these vents from doing their work. Gable vents should be sealed.

54 If you can't vent the attic investigate the hot roof theory

As we have already discussed ad nausium, the attic insulation and venting requirements in all the residential building codes are based on the cold roof theory. Unfortunately, when there is not enough ventilation because of a lack of soffit vents or other restrictions, or when the attic is used for storage and cannot be kept icy cold during the winter, nor allowed to be blazing hot during the summer, the cold roof theory doesn't work.

Also when heat from the house escapes into the attic, the deck boards become heated, roof snow and ice melt and refreeze at the soffit line creating roof dams. These in turn often lead to water damage in the attic and walls of the house.

The hot roof theory was developed in an attempt to find a solution to these problems. Under the hot roof theory all attic ventilation is stopped and the roof is isolated from the attic and the rest of the house with a thick coat of Icynene or other spray foam. Attic walls are also sprayed to keep outside cold or heat from entering the attic.

Icynene is usually the preferred foam for this application because if a roof leak develops, it allows water to pass through the insulating material.

The hot roof theory warms the attic but is hard on shingles
Using the hot roof theory the attic assumes the ambient temperature of the house below. During the winter the roof deck and
shingles attain the exact same temperature as the outside air and
roof dams are eliminated. No heated household air escapes through
the roof into the atmosphere. This keeps the house warmer in
winter.

Using the hot air technique roofs,
gables and soffits are insulated with
spray foam completely blocking
traditional air infiltration patterns.
The attic assumes the ambient
temperature of the house.

*Photo courtesy of Icynene Insulation
System © Icynene, Inc. 2002*

During the summer, no solar heat is permitted to enter the house
from the roof. This keeps the house cooler. The only drawback is
that, since there is no venting from underneath the deck boards to
cool the underside of the shingles, the shingles are exposed to the
full extent of the sun's rays. This can cause premature aging of
asphalt and fiberglass shingles.

Premature shingle aging is not really much of a factor because not
having sufficient attic insulation also causes the aging in addition
to promoting water damage. For my money you are much better off
losing five years of shingle life and eliminating the possibility of
water damage caused by roof damming.

As it stands, the vast majority of houses in the United States and
Canada have been built utilizing the cold roof theory. Unfortunately as heating systems become evermore efficient, it is almost
impossible to stop the migration of heat from the house into the
attic. The DOE is calling for more and more attic insulation and
there is often not enough space at the roofline to pack sufficient
insulation to stop roof dam formation.

The hot roof theory was first developed in the Southern United States as a way to make air conditioning more effective. The theory then migrated North as a possible cure to the ice dam / water damage problem. It may work. So far we have not sufficient experience to recommend switching from the cold roof to the hot roof theory.

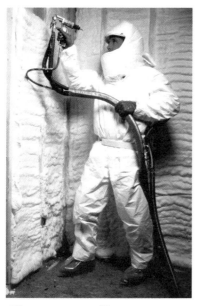

Photo courtesy of Icynene
Insulation System
(c) Icynene, Inc. 2002

The leading proponent of the hot roof theory are the makers of Icynene. They have developed a large body of research on the subject in conjunction with scientists at the Oakridge National Laboratories.

If you have an attic that must be used for storage, insulating it using the hot roof theory would seem a very practical choice. The only problem is that you have to remove everything from the attic while the Icynene or other foam insulation is applied. This could be a lot of work, but at this point in time, there is no effective alternative.

Chapter IV
Security

55 Simple ways to burglar-proof your house

The simple way to cut burglaries by almost 50 percent is to lock your windows and doors, trim the shrubs, put ladders inside the house and stop hiding a key under the mat. The first choice of burglars is to walk through an unlocked door. They aren't picky. They'll go through a front, side, back, breezeway or garage doors. So when I say lock doors, I mean all of them.

The burglar's second choice is a convenient, ground level window. They especially like windows that are hidden by trees or shrubs so that no one can see them going in. If you don't like uninvited guests, trim back the shrubs. Remember that an unattended ladder is an open invitation for someone to climb into an unlocked second-story window. Stop hiding a key outside. If you can find the key, the burglar probably can also.

Next, look at the exterior lights. Standard bulbs burn out too often. If you have carriage or post lights, upgrade to something like GE's 75-watt Teflon-coated post lamp. The bulb is designed to stand up to cold and wet. Put it in now and you won't be freezing your fingers trying to change the bulb in an ice-covered lamppost this winter.

How about installing two or three Halogen flood lights and lighting the front, back and driveway? If you want to go high tech, your local hardware, home center, lighting or electronics store has a wide variety of lamp styles, including those with light sensors that turn on automatically when it gets dark, and motion detectors, that turn on when anyone gets near the house. Of course, lighting and security gear, are only good as long as you have electricity or the back-up batteries are functioning.

How do burglars get in?

#		
#1	Front Door	34%
#2	1st Floor Windows	23%
#3	Back Door	22%
#4	Garage Door	9%
#5	Unlocked Entrances & Storage Areas	6%
#6	Basement	4%
#7	2nd Floor Windows	2%

We make it way to easy!

Make sure that you have canceled the newspaper and made arrangements with a friendly neighbor to pick up the mail and cut the grass or shovel the snow. Upgrade locks on doors and windows. Cylindrical, key-in-knob locks are easy to force open by even an amateur burglar. Doors should have deadbolt locks with a minimum 1-1/2-inch bolt. Make sure that all windows, especially on the ground floor, have good, secure locks, not just the skimpy variety installed by most window manufacturers. Sash locks on double hung windows, which use a nail or screw through the top of the bottom window into the bottom of the upper window frame, can prevent the window from being forced. All sliding and track windows and doors should have broom handles or bars in the track that will prevent opening even if the rather fragile lock is broken.

The American National Standards Institute (ANSI) grades locks. The ratings appear on lock packaging. Grade 1 locks offer good protection and are designed for light commercial and home use. Grade 3 locks are designed for light residential applications, bedroom or bathroom doors, etc. Make sure your exterior doors are Grade 2 or better. If it's time to shop for a new deadbolt lock, check to see that the hardened steel bolt is at least 1 inch long; the lock is of all metal construction (plastic parts can be melted); and the cylinder ring spins.

Illustration courtesy of M.A.G. Engineering & Manufacturing, Inc.

Even a good deadbolt can be kicked in by a pro, but you can make your door almost kickproof. M.A.G. Engineering & Manufacturing, Inc. makes a series of brass and steel lock reinforcers, strike and latch guards.

The brass lock reinforcer is a U-shaped channel that fits over the door and makes it almost kickproof. Adding a security strike plate reinforces the frame and maximizes the protective power of the door.

Photo courtesy of M.A.G. Engineering & Manufacturing, Inc.

M.A.G. also makes a complete line of extra-sturdy patio door locks and window security devices. M.A.G. lock reinforcers are available at most home centers.

56 Add a little high tech to home security

Imagine you're sitting at home watching TV. Somebody drives into your driveway, or walks up to the front door, and they instantly appear on picture in a picture on your TV screen. If you can't recognize them in the small picture, you just push a button and their image covers the screen.

Imagine you're sitting at the office during a blizzard and worry that the power might be cut to your home or to a cottage. You call the empty house and get a complete report, everything is fine: the electricity is on, the sump pump is working, and the temperature is currently 60 degrees.

Imagine you're home alone and hear a noise in the middle of the night, you just press a button and every light inside and outside the house goes on. Then, if you hear another sound and are frightened, you just press the button again and all the lights outside the house start flashing, a siren wails, your bedroom door automatically locks, and the police are called.

Imagine you're soaking up some sun in Florida and the sump pump back home stops working; your house automatically calls up to four friends and tells them about the problem so that it gets fixed before any damage is done.

Imagine your house is empty when an intruder breaks in, and the house calls you and the police and tells you about it. Then the video terminals turn on the VCR, and videotapes the intruder as he moves from room to room. If you have a TV in your office, your house can turn on your office TV and transmit the live action from your home.

If the intruder cuts the electric and phone lines, your house automatically calls police on a hidden cellular phone and tells them what is happening.

Imagine that the same technology turns the lights on and off as you move from room to room; turns your Jacuzzi on while you're driving home; locks all the doors and turns on the security system when you tell it "good night"; makes the breakfast coffee and turns on the lights and radio to wake you in the morning; and precisely monitors your heating and cooling, turning down the heat when you're away, or asleep, warning you not to turn on the dishwasher during expensive peak load periods, and saving you all sorts of money on utility bills.

These things are not dreams they are affordable realities
All this technology is already here and it's a bargain. Most people could have a good system installed in their home for $2.00 a square foot. The hidden cellular phone would cost about $300.00 extra. The number of black and white and color video cameras would alter the price, but all are affordable.

If you are a senior, or live alone, you can have a pendant or monitor that is wired for sound and will automatically call up to four different people if you push the button. Once pushed, the monitor keeps calling until one of the people responds. There can be different programming for when you are home and when you are away and the house is empty.

Passive motion and heat detectors can be paired with sound detectors, which only go off when glass is broken or wood splintered. The reason for the affordability of the new systems is the advent of Power Line Carrier, or X-10, technology which permits controllers to be plugged into wall sockets and send signals over existing 110 wiring.

This means that most of the expensive wiring is already done. Only switches and modules have to be installed. X-10 technology is not just for new homes. It is very easy to install in existing homes. You can have as much or as little of the home monitored as desired. Some people just want to check the sump pump and furnace. Others want to be able to turn on the heat and lights at a cottage from the car phone.

Once a house has been equipped for telephone monitoring, control modules can be given instructions from any telephone, anywhere. Most X-10 systems are installed by contractors but they can be installed by the Do-It-Yourselfer.

Basic X-10 kits are available at electronics stores such as Best Buy for Do-It-Yourselfers. Radio Shack has a Plug 'n Power system. Or you can call X-10 (USA) Inc., (800) 675-3044. Home security is more affordable with the advent of new technology.

57 Put your home in dry-dock before going on vacation

Whether its is a business trip, a much needed vacation, a honeymoon, or a not wanted but never-the-less necessary trip to the hospital, everybody goes somewhere, sometime. What should you do before you leave?

Here's a checklist of things you should do to make sure your house is there to greet you when you return.

BEFORE YOU LEAVE "TO DO" LIST

1. Get a Guardian Angel to look after your house while you are gone. Make a list of people that he or she should call in the event of an emergency. If you have an alarm system, make sure that your home's Guardian Angel knows the codes and that the alarm company knows that you are going on vacation and your designated checker will be entering the house several times a week. They should also have his or her name and phone number.

   Make certain that your home's Guardian Angel knows how to contact you anytime there is a problem and set up a regular communications schedule. Don't rely on the Angel to call you. Tell him or her that you will "call every Sunday to make sure that everything is all right."

2. Walk around the exterior of your house and make certain that there is nothing obviously wrong on your home's roof, windows and walls and grounds. Don't say, "I'll fix it when I get back". Whatever is wrong will get worse while you are gone. A small problem can become a disaster in two or three months. Fix it now.

3. Give friends, relatives and neighbors all your consumables. One power outage can turn frozen meat into muck. Refrigerators often become mold gardens. Get rid of anything that can go bad.

4. Make certain that batteries in smoke detectors are fresh.

5. Cancel newspapers and change addresses on magazines and bills or make provisions for the mail to be picked up at least every other day.

6. Make certain that all utility bills are paid (having the heat turned off while you are gone can be a bummer).

7. Arrange for snow removal (grass cutting in summer).

On the evening before or the day you leave:

8. Install timer switches on radios, TVs and lights. Radios should be turned to talk stations. Make the light and sound move quickly from place to place throughout the day so that it looks and sounds like your daily activity.

9. Put your house on a low water diet. Turn the dial on the water heater down to low (it is even better to turn off the water supply, empty the water tank and turn the gas or electricity to the water heater off) and turn off the water to the washing machine and dishwasher.

10. Take pets and plants to pre-arranged neighbors kennels.

11. Turn thermostat down to 60 degrees. If you turn it lower, the furnace humidifier won't work and wood flooring and furniture will dry out. Check your furnace warranty for details.

12. Remember, nobody really likes citrus candy, so make sure you write yourself a note to send oranges or some other considerate gift to your home's Guardian Angel, in addition to the payment provisions you have already made.

Have a great time. You deserve it.

58   How to pick a Guardian Angel

If you were lucky enough to be going on vacation, it would be nice to think that you could leave your responsibilities behind. Unfortunately if your house is getting cantankerous before you left, it will be very prone to have problems while you are away.

That being the case you have to delegate someone to take over your homeowner duties. The responsibility stays with the homeowner, but the eternal vigilance has to be delegated.

I know that most of you are already saying, "I've got that taken care of. My brother, Joe; or my daughter, Sue, or Harry across the street look in on things once in a while."

There are three problems with this scenario:

1. They may not really have the time but are too nice or too soft hearted to turn you down.

2. They may not be responsible people. Just because a person is a relative does not mean they have enough time or the desire to fulfill a time-consuming job.

3. "Once in a while" often means "almost never" or "whenever I have nothing else to do."

Be honest, how conscientious were you the last time you agreed to check up on someone else's house?

It is your duty as a homeowner to recruit the most conscientious person you know to look after your house when you leave for any extended period of time.

Many aren't up to the job. A young mother with three kids is a perfect example of someone you should not choose. This holds true even if she is your only child.

Old Mrs. Crotchety down the street who glares at you every time you are a little late bringing in your garbage cans on collection day might be a far better choice. A young mother doesn't have any time. Mrs. Crotchety has too much time and spends most of it sticking her nose into other people's business. Perfect!

You were made for each other!

59 Guardian Angel home checklist

Looking out for someone's house while they are away is an awesome responsibility. Hopefully everything will be fine, but if something happens you may have to contact them immediately. Make certain that you have all contact information and all the keys you need to check the house, grounds and garage thoroughly. This is not prying, it is what you must do to be a "Guardian Angel".

At a minimum you need: the homeowner's out-of-town address and phone number; the local police and fire department's phone number; the alarm company (if any) that is protecting the home; the insurance carrier, Home Owners policy number and the name and phone number of the insurance agent; the names and phone numbers of the nearest neighbors and the closest friend or relative that can be relied upon to help if the house has a problem.

GUARDIAN ANGEL CHECKLIST

1. Make a commitment to check the home at least 3-times a week. That sounds like a lot but minor water damage can cause almost irreparable harm in as little as 72 hours.

2. Check the outside of the house to make certain that there have been no mail or package deliveries or any obvious exterior problems.

3. Check electric clocks to make certain that there has not been a power outage since your last visit.

4. Make sure that no electric bulb that is suppose to be burning has burned out. Replace bulbs if necessary. Also check that the radios are still dialed to the correct stations.

5. Check walls and ceilings for signs of water intrusion.

6. Check Thermostat to make certain that it is not flashing a problem signal.

7. Check to see that all faucets are turned off and not leaking.

8. Flush toilets and make certain that the flushing cycle has been completed before you leave.

9. Once a month, pour a cup of water into the automatic dishwasher to keep the seals moist.

10. Go downstairs and double-check the furnace and humidifier.

11. Change the lighting pattern of the lights that are on timers so that it looks like someone is really there.

12. Give closets a "sniff test". If the odor is bad, there is a problem. Find out what it is.

Discuss this list with the homeowners before they leave. They may have some critical need, such as feeding a cat or goldfish, which I have not included here.

60   How to make your house child proof

Speaking as grand parents, Barbara and I can tell you that there is no greater joy than having the grandchildren come to stay for a little while. But it is an awesome responsibility.

If you have not had tiny tots around your house for a while and it is not already childproof, making your home a safe place is your most important do-it-yourself project.

Look at your house from a baby's point of view
One of your first projects should be walking around the house on your knees to see your home's dangers from a child's point-of-view. You will be surprised at the sharp corners, electrical cords and dangerous or breakable objects you will discover. Use this checklist to eliminate the most obvious dangers.

Child safety checklist

1. Store cleaning supplies, household chemicals, medications and purses where they can not be reached.
2. Install covers over electrical outlets.
3. Cover sharp edges on furniture.
4. Install screw-in safety gates at stairways.
5. Close off unused rooms.
6. Make sure that curling irons and electrical cords are out of reach.
7. Keep pets and children separated.
8. Have a child-safe play pen on hand.
9. Install night lights in bedrooms, baths, and hallways.
10. Hang a towel over the bathroom door so it can not be completely closed.
11. Put alarm bells on doorknobs.
12. Don't take pills in front of small children.
13. Don't boil water on front stove burners.
14. Place pans on stovetop with handles pointing toward the wall.

Now relax and enjoy yourself.

61 Things you need to have in the house in case of emergency

1. Fire Extinguishers, at least 3. One in the kitchen, one in the master bedroom and one in the basement.
2. Carbon monoxide detectors, 2 or more. One in the basement, one on each floor, one in the bedroom hallway.
3. Smoke detectors in every bedroom, main hallway, by furnace, and at least one on every floor of the house.
4. Pressure balancing or anti scald devices such as those made by MemrySafe and PPP Inc. distributed by Tech Results Inc. Put one in the kitchen and every bathroom sink, shower and tub.
5. A Magne Flo Excess Flo Valve - - EFV should be installed directly after the gas main. In the event of a gas leak, this inexpensive device will shut the gas off before a potentially lethal condition exists. Magne Flo EFV valves can be installed at both the main gas line and at all major gas appliances for extra security.
6. Automatic water shut off devices such as the Wags Water heater Shut Off Valve or Great Bay Products FloLogic system 2000, which are designed to protect an entire home from severe water damage.
7. Lighting and security motion detectors.
8. Water powered back-up sump pump if the house is on city water. Use a battery powered back up sump pump if on well water.
9. Whole house surge protectors for electric, cable and phone lines.

John Paul Jones-Stief, the executive in charge of Office and Internet Security at Master Handyman Press, wanted me to remind you that Man's Best Friend is also the best security device known to man. A dog will not only bark and scare away the bad guys, he or she will lick your face, take you for walks and give you an unlimited supply of love and devotion.

If you don't have a dog, you can easily find one or two that would make perfect companions at the nearest dog pound or animal shelter. Consider adopting an older dog. They are usually house broken and very adaptable. Besides, you will literally be saving a life. That can make big points for you with the Big Guy Upstairs.

OK Jonsie, can I go back to writing the book now?

Chapter V
Plumbing

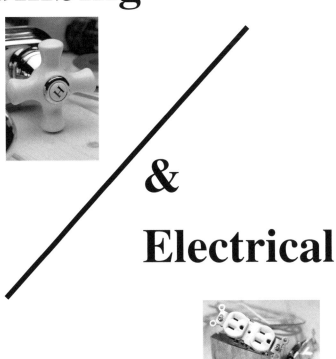

& Electrical

62 Upgrading the water supply on a new home will solve a lot of future problems

Given a choice, most builders put in the minimum the building code allows. I talk a great deal about Code Plus construction. Here are a few of my Code Plus suggestions for your water supply.

You can use many of these ideas to upgrade the water service to your present home. All you need to do is find a plumber who wants to bring your home into the 21st Century.

Most homes have 3/4-inch diameter pipes connecting to the city water lines bringing water into the house. Water is a critical need

for the proper functioning of toilets, showers and faucets. A good way to solve future problems is to upgrade to 1-inch diameter pipe. This small increase dramatically increases the amount of water available to the house at any given time.

If water pressure is a problem in your community, include an in-line water pressure-boosting pump like the Davey XP and HS series, to improve the flow.

In our Code Plus house, we will call for all hot and cold water lines to be copper. In some parts of the country which have water with very low pH and high CO2, high quality CPVC pipe, such as FlowGuard Gold, would be preferred. In the vast majority of the country, however, copper is the quality standard.

All the water that comes in has to go out. The drain waste vents and pipes will be iron. PVC pipes and fittings are less expensive and easier to install. They are also less substantial and more prone to have problems.

63 A recirculating pump can save you money and give instantly hot water

The average family pours 7,000 to 14,000 gallons of water down the drain every year waiting for the water to turn hot. This wastes water, time and money. The problem is easy to solve, but because it is an extra cost item, and plumbers are not sales people, they don't bother to tell you about it.

The way to eliminate water waste is to install a recirculating pump that senses when the hot water turns cold and replaces it with more hot water.

There are two different types of recirculating pump systems. The Nibco Just Right pump requires a special water line to return the cooled water to the hot water tank.

The second type of recirculating pump eliminates the need for a return line by directing the cooled water to into the cold water line. The Grundfos Pumps' Comfort Pump uses a special value located at the farthest sink to transfer the cooled water. The Laing Thermotech Instant Hot Water Pump, is located under the farthest sink and sends the cooled water into the cold water line.

The primary difference between the Grundfos and the Laing systems is that the Grundfos pump is located near the hot water tank and requires electric power at the tank site. The Laing pump is located under the sink farthest away from the hot water tank and is plugged into an electrical outlet at that site. If you only have two electric outlets at that location you might have to have another outlet installed.

64 Take control of the water you drink

Let's face it. Many people do not like the taste of the water they drink. Tap water is often so treated with so many chemicals that the smell alone makes you want to stay away from the stuff. An increasing amount of people use bottled water as an alternative. Unfortunately many bottled waters are no better than that which we can get from the tap.

A good solution is to take the water that the water department provides, and then re-process it to come up to your standards.

Two types of water purification systems
There are two different types of household water purification — whole house and point of use. A whole house system treats all the water used in the house. A point of use system is a filter attached to the dispensing device. Whole house systems are the way to go for people with wells and, in special cases, for people with city water.

Most of us on city water will find point-of-use filters fit our requirements. A filter system directly connected to the kitchen sink will cover 90 percent of the family's water consumption for cooking and drinking, but would not provide any help removing the chlorine from the shower water. If you are sensitive to chlorine, you will be better off with a whole house system.

If you want the best water ask an expert
Whenever I want to know about water, I talk to Nick DiSalvio of Environmental Water Service. To DiSalvio, water treatment is not a business, it is a vocation. When I asked DiSalvio about point-of-use filters, he said that there were two types: true filters and reverse osmosis (RO) systems.

The first is the most common and is what most people think of when they talk about a filter. It attaches directly under the kitchen counter, or stands on top of the counter. It may be attached to the faucet, or may include a special faucet just for the treated water.

This type of filter can have many types of filter inserts, is made by many different manufacturers, and comes in many different price ranges. The most effective filters are made of activated carbon. For instance the Culligan UC-1A filter has a 1,500-gallon capacity and protects against lead, cryptosporidium and giardia bacteria, chlorine, and improves taste and odor. Filters must be replaced every 1,500 gallons. If this is not done, filtration stops and previously filtered impurities may actually be added to the drinking water.

A hybrid of this type combines a carbon filter with UV and ozone. Ozone, like chlorine, is a powerful oxidizer and destroys contaminants. UV destroys the bacteria and viruses. The activated carbon filter traps lead, chlorine, etc. UV/carbon filters are made by several manufacturers. The filter made by Alpine Industries uses a process called photo-oxidation to make the UV and Ozone even more effective.

Reverse osmosis is a good defense against carcinogens
Although very effective, carbon based filters can't be effective against carcinogens like arsenic or nitrates. To protect yourself against these types of problems, choose an RO system. An RO system uses reverse osmosis to purify water. A good RO system, like the Hydrotech, distributed by Environmental Water Systems, processes about 45 gallons of drinking water a day. In an RO system, surplus water washes away impurities and very little maintenance is needed.

Whole house water purification systems use a combination of filters and water treatments, to create the final product. City water may just need super-sized carbon filters. If additional purification is required, adding an ultra violet light may do the trick. DiSalvio prefers to use water purification systems that use hydrogen peroxide to totally destroy all the contaminants, then a series of filters, a water softener and a RO system for drinking water.

65 Keep baby and grandma safe from scalds

Water heated over 114° F can scald a person. Up to 30% of all burn injuries may be scald related. An especially large number of infants, elderly and disabled people suffer horrible burns every year.

This usually happens because the very young or older people have lower sensitivity and/or slower reaction time than the rest of the population.

If the water gets really hot it doesn't take more than a second or two to get a burn that you will carry with you for the rest of your life. Yaun Co., a large plumbing and heating distributor keeps the following chart on their web site to educate their customers on the need for anti-scald devices.

Second and Third Degree Burn Chart

Water Temp F	Time for 1st Degree Burn	Time for 2nd or 3rd Degree burn
111.2	5 hours	7 hours
116.6	35 minutes	45 minutes
118.4	10 minutes	14 minutes
122.0	1 minute	5 minutes
131.0	5 seconds	25 seconds
140.0	2 seconds	5 seconds
149	1 second	2 secconds
158	less than 1 second	1 second

Source: Johns Hopkins University

It doesn't matter if you are young or old, if you are going to use water heated above 114° F, some type of anti scalding device should be placed in all faucet and shower fixtures in both the kitchen and all bathrooms.

Products like Sparco Aquamix, MemrySafe and PPP Inc. Anti-Scald Devices distributed by Tech Results Inc, and many others can do the job.

According to Tech Results over 35,000 children under 14 years of age are treated for scalding at emergency wards each year.

MemrySafe® and PPP Inc. Anti-Scald Devices belong to a new product category known as Temperature Actuated Flow Reduction Valves or "TAFRs". TAFRs are point-of-use devices that fit into individual plumbing fixtures, such as shower heads; bath and utility faucets; and sink and lavatory faucets.

MemrySafe® and PPP Inc. Anti-Scald Devices do not require a plumber and can be installed by a home-owner as a retro-fit accessory in less than one hour. These devices provide complete scald protection for all discharge outlets including: showers, sink faucets, and bathtubs.

MemrySafe® and PPP Inc. Anti-Scald Devices are non-electrical temperature-sensitive, not pressure-sensitive devices. They do not mix or adjust the water temperature, but reduce water flow to a trickle of less than 1/4 gallon per minute when the water temperature exceeds 120°F at the point of discharge.

These devices are activated as a result of either too much hot water being used or the cold water pressure having dropped. They then automatically resume full flow when the temperature reaches a safe level of approximately 98°F. When the unit senses dangerous scalding water, it immediately reduces the flow to a trickle. When the scalding temperature subsides, the unit automatically resumes normal flow.

Many manufacturers also make faucets and showerheads with anti-scalding adapters built into them.

If you retro fit your present fixtures or buy new scald proof fixtures you can have all the hot water you need for sanitation and not have to worry about accidental scalding from accidental immersion in very hot water.

66   Put a stop to phantom flushes

Leaking toilets waste as much or more water than leaking faucets, but you can have a toilet problem and not know about it. Alternatively the family may all be in the family room or eating dinner in the kitchen and a toilet at the far end of the house may flush.

This phenomenon is called the phantom flush. It is not a sign of ghosts, but of a flapper ball that has deteriorated to the point where it is allowing water to escape from the tank to the bowl. When sufficient water leaks into the bowl, it flushes.

This problem is happening with increasing frequency because the various water departments are putting in a great deal more chlorine and other chemicals into the water supply. Also most toilet bowl tablets that you leave inside the water tank are chlorine-based and attack the flapper ball and corrode metal parts in the toilet.

Water tank test
It is very easy to test your toilets to see if they are leaking. Take a bottle of really ugly food coloring into the toilet, lift the tank lid and flush the toilet. Once the tank has emptied completely and is beginning to refill, pour the food coloring into the water tank and let it sit for ten minutes.

After the time has elapsed, lift the seat of the commode and see if any of the food coloring has leaked into the commode. If it has, it is time to change the flapper ball, the water tank gasket or both.

67 Flapper balls can cost you a fortune

Solving a leaking toilet problem is usually very easy. The cause is usually a flapper ball that no longer seats correctly. Alternatively, it may be that the gasket used to seal the flapper ball may have deteriorated and need to be replaced. If you are uncertain, change both.

There are about 16 different size flapper balls so it is easy to get the wrong size. To make certain you get the correct replacement equipment, write down the toilet manufacturer's name and model number (both are usually on the inside of the water tank cover). Then turn off the water at the toilet and drain the tank.

Take off the flapper ball and take it and the toilet information to a plumbing supply house. Give the counter person the information, and he or she will give you an exact replacement part.

The replacement parts often come in kit form so you get exactly the right gasket for the specific flapper ball. Some manufacturers, like Corkey, have developed new and improved flapper ball materials that are almost impervious to the chlorine and other chemicals in today's water supply.

Most manufacturers are very consumer oriented and include very specific, step-by-step directions in the package.

One final word of advice: when replacing the flapper ball, make sure that the chain linking the commode handle and the flapper ball has just the right amount of tension.

If the chain is too tight the flapper ball may not be able to sit properly, allowing water to escape. Too little tension and the flapper ball may not get picked up fast enough when the handle is turned to allow sufficient water to flow into the commode.

Some toilets, like the Mansfield, use a flush valve instead of a flapper ball to release water to the commode. Flush valves have seals instead of flapper balls. Usually all you have to do to fix a leak is replace the seal. The best place to look for flush valve seals is a plumbing supply store.

68 A leaky faucet can drain your bank account

One of the most vexing, but easy to solve problems is the leaky faucet. Once it starts, you not only hear the relentless drip, drip, drip all night long, all that water that is being wasted costs a heck of a lot of money.

It is estimated that just one leaky faucet can waste 8 to 20 gallons of water a day. That's 3,000 to 7,000 gallons a year.

Luckily, fixing most faucets is simple. The biggest challenges you will face is determining which type of faucet you have and getting the exact replacement parts.

The only tools you will usually need will be a regular screwdriver, a Philips head screwdriver, plumbing pliers, needle nose pliers and, possibly a utility knife. Sometimes a faucet handle is especially hard to pull off. Full service plumbing supply handles have a special tool you can buy to remove the handle.

In the old days there was only one type of faucet. It is called the compression faucet and was usually fixed by replacing the washer at the bottom of the compression fitting.

Now there are three additional types of faucets: rotary ball single lever, cartridge and ceramic disc.

The rotary ball single lever faucet was developed by the founders of the Delta faucet company. It became the largest selling faucet in America and formed the foundation of Masco, a huge international company.

The cartridge faucet is often associated with the Moen faucet company, while many of the better European faucets are ceramic disk.

If you are being economical and have one of the major brand faucets there is a good chance that the faucet has a lifetime guaranty. This doesn't really mean that the faucet is supposed to last a lifetime without leaking. It means that most faucets are changed for design purposes before they leak.

If you keep the faucet long enough and can track down the model number, call the manufacturer's customer relations department and tell them your faucet is leaking. There is a good chance they will send you the replacement parts free.

If you are like most of us and either don't want to bother waiting a couple of weeks for the parts to arrive in the mail, or hire a plumber to do the work, you will wind up paying for the replacement parts.

Get the right parts and a faucet is easy to fix. Many of the replacement kits have very good step by step instructions so once you have the right parts doing the job is not much of a challenge.

One word of warning if you have a very inexpensive, imported knock-off faucet you may not be able to find the proper size replacement parts. In fact there may not be any. On the other hand, you may be able to buy a whole new faucet for the price of an expensive faucet replacement kit.

To make certain that you get the proper parts, turn off the water leading to the faucet then take off the cap at the top of the faucet handle. When the cap is removed, unscrew the Philips screw that attaches the handle to the faucet. Remove the handle and unscrew the decorative fitting that covers the working parts of the faucet.

On an expensive faucet this part is usually very shiny and may even be gold or silver plated. The best way to remove it is with ChannelLock's toothless adjustable pliers. If you don't have or can't get the toothless kind, wrap a thick piece of cloth around the fixture before using the pliers.

To repair a compression faucet all you usually have to do is replace the worn washer that is attached to the bottom of the stem with a screw.

You should also replace the O-Ring or in much older faucets the string packing. If the valve seat is rough it can be smoothed out with a seat cutter that you can buy at any plumbing supply or hardware store.

To repair a rotary ball faucet, replace the housing seal, valve seats and springs as well as the O-ring, washer and cam.

To repair a cartridge faucet you usually only have to replace the O-ring, cartridge and clip.

Ceramic Disk faucets seldom leak because the ceramic disks grind up minerals that can wear other types of faucets. If a ceramic disk faucet does leak the cartridge has to be replaced.

Whichever type of faucet you have the procedure you use to fix it should be the same. Take the faucet apart, then take the faucet's internal parts with you to the plumbing supply store.

If you are replacing a cartridge and O-Rings you have to replace it with the identical part. Don't trust yourself on this. Go to the counter, show the person the part and tell them the make and, if possible, the model number of the faucet. He or she will give you the proper repair kit. While you are there, ask if he has any tips on that type of repair.

When you get home open the package carefully and read the instructions. The trickiest part is often removing and replacing the O-Rings.

Once you have all the parts the job itself shouldn't take more than 20 minutes. Be careful to re-assemble the faucet in the exact order that you took it apart.

69 The care, feeding and eventual replacement of your hot water heater

The hot water tank is a silent servant. It just sits there and does its job. We don't usually think about it. Here are a few things you should think about.

Water tank temperature

A hot water tank set at medium should heat the water in the tank to about 120° Fahrenheit (F). A lot of well-intentioned people say that is too high and say that you should dial down the water temperature for energy conservation and safety.

Unfortunately it has been discovered that Legionella bacteria thrive at 120°. If you want to keep your hot water tank safe from Legionella the temperature has to be at least 140°.

Whether 120° F is too high, too low, or just about right depends on what you want the water to do.

If you don't like germs and want to sterilize clothing or dishes you need a water temperature of 140° F. If you or someone in your family has asthma or allergies and want to kill the dust mites in your bedclothes you need a temperature of 130° F.

If you want the water in the washing machine to be130° F it needs to be about 140° in the water tank because water cools as it goes through the pipes and cascades into the washer.

If you have a 40-gallon hot water tank and you and your significant other each like to take ten-minute showers at the same time, one of you will probably run out of warm water if the hot water tank was not set at a minimum of 120° F.

Maintenance:

Most of us never think about our home's hot water heater until, or unless we run out of hot water. Although it takes the very smallest amount of maintenance, we usually do not do even that. Then we scream with outrage when the water heater fails to perform.

PlumbingSupply.com, one of the big plumbing web sites, recommends that both electric and gas water heaters be drained until the water is clear at least once every three months. Here are their step-by-step instructions.

1. If the water heater is electric, shut-off the electricity.
2. If the water heater is gas, turn down the gas valve to off.
3. Shut-off the cold water intake to the heater.
4. Open a hot water faucet on any level above the water heater.
5. Open the bottom drain valve at the bottom of your water heater.
6. Drain enough water so that the water runs clear.
7. Shut the water faucet that you opened
8. Open the cold water intake valve.
9. Run all the faucets in the house till no more air is sputtering out for at least 10 seconds.
10. Turn electricity/gas back on.

© *since 1995 PlumbingSupply.com*

Mineral Buildup:

Mineral buildup sometimes causes rumbling, crackling or popping sound in the hot water heater. This sound is associated with mineral buildup. The popping sound is caused by water trapped under lime deposits escaping or being boiled away when trapped above the heating element.

Tri Brothers Chemical Corp. produces a product called Mag-Erad. This product dissolves the mineral buildup so that it can be flushed from the tank. The project takes about two hours, according to the water-heating specialists at Hartford and Ratliff.

Hartford and Ratliff sends the product nationwide. Two containers are needed for a 30- or 40-gallon water heater and three containers for a 40- to 60-gallon water heater. If you have an older water heater you may need more Mag-Erad to do the job.

This project is quite labor intensive and Mag-Erad is quite costly. If you are going to do the job yourself, the job is worth doing. If you are going to hire a plumber to do it you have to weigh the pros and cons about whether it is time to get a new hot water heater.

Replacement:
Here are a couple other indications that it may be time to start shopping for a new heater.

If the water does not get very hot
Most water heaters are gas fired at the bottom of the tank. Over the years, rust, flaking, and scaling of calcium and magnesium build-up, and sediment from water born impurities settle to the bottom of the tank, insulating the water from the heat. As the sediment builds, the heater becomes less and less efficient.

If the hot water tank is ten or fifteen years old
The harder the water, the shorter the tank's life expectancy. Some hot water tanks last only seven years.

If you have to call a plumber a couple of times
If you have had to call a plumber in to fix your water heater a couple of times or if he suggests a repair that will cost over $100.

Here's a test you can use to see if your hot water tank is operating efficiently.

Check to see if the water heater temperature setting is at medium. Attach a garden hose to the hot water drain.

Fill the laundry tub full of hot water. Don't put the stopper in until hot water is coming out. The average tub holds about 26 gallons of water.

Test the temperature with a meat thermometer. Do not, under any circumstances put your bare hand into this water. You can get a scald burn at 114° Fahrenheit (F). The water in the laundry tub will be considerably higher.

If the hot water tank is operating efficiently, the temperature of the entire tub of water should be at least 120° F. If it is much lower, you either have the water heater set too low, or the tank is no longer heating efficiently and should be replaced.

If it is much above 120° F, the setting of this high temperature should have been a conscious decision on your part. Although your washer and dishwasher operate more efficiently with water at 140° F, a setting of only 120° F is the recommended industry standard for safety reasons .

If you decide that it is time to replace your hot water heater, I would suggest that you increase its size and efficiency. Government regulations have changed the efficiency and the way water heaters are rated.

It now takes a rapid recovery 50-gallon water heater to provide the same amount of water that a standard 40-gallon water heater used to provide.

That means that if there are 2 or more of you in the family, you need a 50-gallon water heater with a rating of 50,000 BTUs. Some of the big box chains I have checked do not carry rapid recovery 50-gallon water heaters. In fact at the last big box store I checked, their best 50-gallon water heater had the same first hour recovery rate as their best 40-gallon water heater.

If you have a family with 2 or 3 kids (especially girls) who like to take long showers and spend a lot of time on washing their hair, seriously consider investing in a 75-gallon water heater.

How much hot water do you really need?
Here's a handy chart that tells approximately how much water various appliances will use in a minute. If you multiply how many appliances may be going at the same time by the number going at once, you can determine how many minutes operating time you will have before the hot water runs out.

To complicate things a little we often use 50 to 70% hot water and 30 to 50% cold water. It all depends on your comfort level. If you like hot showers you run out of hot water sooner. Some 50-gallon hot water heaters only have a first hour rate of 86 gallons. Four people taking 10-minute showers can play havoc with the hot water supply.

Water Usage

Appliance	Gallons per Minute Minimum	Gallons per Minute Maximum
Bath Sink	1.5	2.5
2 Bath Sinks	3	5
Shower	2	3.5
2 Showers	4	7
Bath Tub	2	3
Washing Machine	4	6
Dishwasher	2	3
Kitchen Sink	2.5	3

70 What you need to know before you buy a tankless water heater

Going tankless can be thankless

Tankless water heaters sound like a wonderful idea. You stop wasting money heating and storing water and save energy which is very energy efficient. They are very popular in Europe and the Orient where people are a great deal more energy conscious than we are.

Unfortunately most water heaters are single appliance products. If you take a shower at the same time that someone else is doing the laundry, you will both run out of hot water.

If you buy a powerful enough tankless water heater to fit the needs of an average American household, you are going to invest a good deal more money than you would pay for a conventional water tank system. A tankless water heater powerful enough to handle 3 fixtures at a time will average about $2,000 in product and installation costs.

The Rinnai of America Continuum tankless hot water heater supplies up to 8.5 gallons per minute. The Bosch AquaStar Model 240 FX delivers up to 5 gallons per minute, enough to supply two major appliances.

71 Put a stop to sewer gas and toilet talk back

When the toilet starts gurgling or there is a sewer gas smell in the bathroom it usually means that the sanitary stack vent is probably clogged. The sanitary stack vent is the little pipe on the top of your roof that equalizes the air pressure in the drains and keeps the plumbing running smoothly.

A house should have one sanitary stack for every two toilets. If you have a third toilet you should have two sanitary stack vents.

As the years go by leaves and twigs drop down the vent stack and block the plumbing's air supply. A gurgling in the bathroom or a sewer gas smell is usually an indication that the vent needs cleaning.

This is not a do-it-yourself job. Call a drain-cleaning company and tell them that you need to have the sanitary stack vents on your roof snaked out. Not every plumbing company does this kind of work. Many drain cleaners do not like crawling on top of a roof, especially during the winter. It is best to tell the person scheduling appointments what you need so that you can be sure that the company does that kind of work before they make a service call.

If you had sewer gas odor, after the sanitary stack vent has been snaked out, go to the hardware store and get some copper sulfate crystals. Mix 12 ounces of the crystals in 1 gallon of hot water, and pour it slowly down the drain.

Let it stand two hours, then flush with 5 gallons of cold water. The smell will be gone for good. Brag about it.

72 Need to know info on sump pumps

Sump pumps come in three different styles: pedestal, submersible and torpedo. The pedestal sump pump's motor is out of the water and actuated by a ball cock mechanism. The submersible sump pump is located inside the sump crock. The torpedo style sump pump is most commonly used when a house was not originally built with a sump, and is in the drain tile cleanout.

All of these pumps are actuated by a rising water level. When the water in the sump rises to a pre-set level, the switch clicks and the pump turns on and pumps the water from the bottom of the sump up a pipe and over to a discharge outlet.

Residential sump pump motors are usually .3 to .5 (1/2) horse power (hp). The Zoeller .3 hp submersible sump pump can pump 34 gallons a minute, or 2040 gallons an hour, up a ten foot lift and get it out of your house. The 1/2 hp submersible model is rated at 61 gallons a minute, or 3660 gallons an hour. Wayne Pump's 1/2 hp submersible is rated at 3000 gallons an hour.

Bigger does not necessarily mean better. In real life, a sump pump almost never runs for an hour. Quite often, it will only run five or ten minutes in five or ten hours and may not even turn on for months at a time. The longer sump pumps run, the more efficient they become. So unless you have a definite need to move a great deal of water, the .3 hp may be a better choice.

Sump pumps are very reliable, easy to maintain, and will serve you for many years. Their switches may have to be changed five or six times during those years. If the switch breaks, the pump won't turn on.

Maintenance:
Many sump pumps are needed only during the wet season. If it has been dry and the sump pump has not functioned for a month or so, it is a good ideal to exercise the sump pump by pouring a couple pails of water into the sump crock. If the pump turns on and pumps the water out, everything is fine. If it does not function the switch may need to be replaced.

The sump pump should also be inspected regularly during the wet season. Look into the sump for debris. Brush off calcium deposits. If you haven't heard the pump go on in a while pour some water into the sump crock to see if the pump goes on. If it doesn't, the switch probably needs to be replaced.

Scoop out the muck from the bottom of the sump at least once a year. A good way to keep the crock clear of accumulated debris is to run a garden hose from your laundry tub and turn on the cold water. This churns up the gunk and gives the pump a chance to get rid of it.

Back Up Sump Pumps:
Since sump pumps are powered by electricity, when the electricity goes out in a storm, the pump stops working when it is needed most. You can install a backup sump pump to guard against a power failure.

Most back up pumps are battery powered. On the better ones, like the Ace In The Hole (so help me, that is the name of the pump and the company that makes it), when the electricity goes out, an alarm sounds and the battery-powered backup starts pumping.

When the power failure is of short duration, everything is fine. As soon as the electricity goes back on, the battery pump stops and the battery recharges. If a power failure lasts for a long time, the battery pumps for about 24 hours. Even installing a second battery attachment just saves the basement for another day.

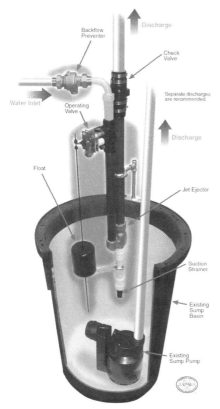

Backflow
Preventer

Discharge

Check
Valve

Separate discharges
are recommended.

Water Inlet

Operating
Valve

Discharge

Float

Jet Ejector

Suction
Strainer

Existing
Sump
Basin

Existing
Sump Pump

Water powered backup sump pump

A completely different kind of backup sump pump, like the Saginaw Guardian by A. Y. McDonald Mfg. Co., uses water power from the city water line. If your house is hooked up to a city system, a water powered backup pump gives unlimited protection. It will keep working as long as the water lines have pressure.

Illustration courtesy of A. Y. McDonald Mfg. Co.

73   How to quiet noisy water pipes

There are two types of sound associated with water pipes: water hammering and the banging associated with air cushion loss.

Water Hammering:

Single lever faucets, some water heaters or the automatic solenoid valves in dishwashers and washing machines often cause a water hammer effect. The faster water valve closes, the greater the intensity of the shock to the pipe along which the water is flowing.

At its worst, the water hammer effect can expand the water tank shell by increasing water pressure in the tank beyond its capacity or collapse the flue tube at the top of the water heater.

The best remedy for this problem is to have your plumber install water hammer arrestors as close to the source of the closure as possible. The arrestors prevent damage by absorbing the shock wave in an air cushion.

Loss of Air Cushion:

After plumbing work is done it is often necessary to reestablish the air cushion to eliminate various rattles and banging in the pipes. This is a one-person job because the steps have to be taken in exact order.

Turn off the water at the water meter then turn off the water supply to each toilet and the washing machine and dishwasher. Go to the sink closest to the water main and turn on the cold water tap. Then go to the sink farthest away from the water main and turn on that cold water tap (If you live in a 2-story house that will be on the second floor).

Let all the water drain out of the system before turning off the top and bottom faucets.

Turn on the water at the meter then open the valves to the toilets and washing machine.

Turn on each hot and cold-water faucet and flush every toilet.

You will hear a lot of banging and spitting as you exercise the faucets and the toilets may sound like they are exploding.
By doing this you will have now re-established the air cushion in your water system and it should operate quietly.

74   Give your home the electric power it needs

Most of the electrical systems in American houses were built for a bygone era, which required far less power. Unfortunately many new houses are not much better because the builder puts in the minimum he can get away with and still meet "Code".

Every time we bring in a bigger sound system or a more advanced coffee maker we increase the load on our wiring. Then we go crazy with outside decorations during the holiday season and wonder why the electricity goes out or, worse, we have an electric fire.

How much power does a new house need?
I asked Don Collins of Budget Electric to outline what he believes is an optimal electrical system for the modern house. Collins is a good choice because his company pulls more residential permits than any other electrical contractor in Michigan and, on a personal level, he recently built the home of his dreams. So he can look at the matter as both a consumer and as an electrical contractor.

Most of the people who read this book will not live in Michigan but the need for more electric power is nation-wide.

Collins started off by telling me to have two 200-amp panels. He also suggested putting in a 100-amp slave panel in a first-floor mudroom so that minor modifications in power needs can be handled easily. That sounded high, but Collins told me that in new home construction you should try to build to suit power requirements for the next 20 years.

"Before the dry wall goes up, putting in some extra electric panels or wiring is relatively cheap. After a home is finished, upgrading wiring can be time-consuming and expensive," he says.

Room by room recommendations for electric power

 Kitchen: This is the most power-hungry room in the house. It needs at least 6 home run (clear) circuits — three circuits for counter appliances and a separate circuit for the dishwasher and garbage disposal as well as a 240-volt circuit for the stove. If you are planning on having multiple electric ovens or disposers, you need one clear circuit for each.

Bathrooms: A basic bathroom needs a 20-amp circuit for the GFI (Ground Fault Interrupter) plugs and another circuit for lighting and bath fan. Collins says it is possible to save a little here because one lighting and bath fan circuit can cover two bathrooms. On the other hand, if you have a powerful jetted tub you may need two clear circuits for that alone. One circuit for the heater, one circuit for the jets.

Arc faults are suspected to cause a significant percentage of the more than 43,000 electrical home fires every year. To protect against arc faults, Eaton Cutler-Hammer (www.cutler-hammer.eaton.com) makes AFCI/GFCI (Arc Fault and Ground Fault Circuit Interrupter) that are like GFI plugs on steroids. These plugs will actually sense if there is any arcing going on in the lines of the house and turn the power off before there is a problem.

Naturally they cost far more than ordinary GFI plugs but you should investigate them and see if you want to invest in the extra protection.

Family room: This room also requires a great deal of power. You need one clear circuit for general lighting, one for recessed lighting and one 15-amp circuit for the entertainment wall. As far as the recessed lighting goes, the rule is one circuit for every five cans. You can easily have more than five recessed lights and would therefore need more than one circuit.

"Many people want to upgrade to a 20-amp circuit for their entertainment wall. I don't think that is a good idea because too much power can burn out the wiring on expensive audio video components. I'd rather have a power drain knock out the breaker on the panel than burn out the equipment," Collins says.

Computer room: This highly specialized room needs one 20-amp circuit for the computer, monitor and printer and one 15-amp for general lighting and convenience plugs.

Bedrooms & miscellaneous rooms: Every room should have a dedicated "home run" (clear) circuit. Bedrooms with therapeutic equipment (a treadmill to a hospital bed) may need a 20-amp circuit to supply the needed power.

Hallways: Collins recommends a 15-amp circuit for lighting and a 20-amp circuit for vacuums and carpet cleaning. "We get calls from people blowing plugs with the new 12-amp vacuums. If they have the vac plugged into a 15-amp circuit and anything else is drawing power from the line, they can easily have a problem. With a 20-amp circuit, there is no problem," he says.

Basement: Collins recommends recessed lighting in the basement. "There is never enough light, so figure one light for every 200 square feet. You will probably need at least one circuit for the lighting and one dedicated circuit for every 8 duplex receptacles (plugs). The basement humidifier requires another circuit. A central vacuum system will also require a dedicated circuit," he said.

Crawl space and attic: Collins recommends a dedicated 15-amp circuit for attic lighting plus another dedicated circuit for power and exhaust fans. The crawl space requires a minimum of one light and a switch.

Throughout the house: Even if you do not have the need today, Collins recommends running Category 5 cable and phone jacks in every room of the house.

Outside: Collins is a fan of recessed lighting in the soffits rather than low-powered ground lighting. He also suggests having plenty of water-proof outside receptacles.

"Remember, you don't just live in the front or the back of the house. You need electrical power availability on all four sides. Also, if your deck is going to be an entertaining center you will need plenty of power for that area. I suggest three or more dedicated outside circuits: one or more for lighting; one for the deck and one for receptacles around the house perimeter."

Since all these things are wonderful they don't do any good if your locality is in the midst of a power black out. For this reason Collins recommends a natural gas or propane generator that will supply minimal power when the electricity goes down, plus phone, cable and electric service surge protectors.

Your home may not require all of these circuits, but you never know how your needs may change and having sufficient power built into your home's electric system will be a big plus when it comes time to sell. Follow these recommendations and you'll always have the power for your electric needs.

Upgrade the electrical in existing homes by adapting new home guidelines. Your television does not make allowances for the fact that you live in a 50-year old home. None of your other electrical appliances are more forgiving. It is therefore a good idea to upgrade your present home to meet the new reality.

Usually you do not have to tear out old wiring when you upgrade. Just bypass the old and add new circuits where needed.

Upgrading the electric panel to at least 200 amps gives most homeowners the extra circuits they need to provide the necessary increase in power.

A line that runs directly from the panel to an area of the house where it is needed is called a "home run." It provides an entire circuit's worth of power at a given location.

You need two home runs in the kitchen, two in the television room, one for all the bathrooms and one for the computer room.

New home runs require that you install new electric receptacles in the given rooms. Be sure to install some of the plugs at waist height following universal design recommendations.

75 Surge protectors keep your appliances from going up in smoke

Electric power is a two-edged sword. It is absolutely essential for modern life, but it can destroy your appliances and burn down your house.

I have been preaching about the need for surge protectors for years and installation cost is very economical. Never the less, the vast majority of our homes are unprotected.

Most problems relating to electricity and electronic devices can be traced to line noise, over-voltage, and under voltage. Examples of over-voltage are spikes and surges. A spike is a very short over-voltage condition, usually less than a millionth of a second. Spikes usually don't harm electronic equipment.

Surges last much longer — usually last several thousandths of a second — and are often more powerful. This, in electronic terms, is long term over-charging. It can overcome internal protection and burn out (fry) delicate electric circuits.

A spike can be created from something as innocuous as one person turning on the electric clothes dryer, while another person is on the computer.

A surge can be created from a squirrel chewing through an electric cable, two or three neighbors turning on their air conditioning at the same time, a lineman shutting off, then returning the power to a line, or lightening hitting a tower and sending a couple of hundred thousand extra volts down the line.

Surges can also be transmitted through the ground for considerable distances and cause a great deal of damage.

In our parent's day, most electrical equipment had manual switches that simply turned off and on. Spikes, surges — even low power situations — seldom caused major damage. With the introduction of ever more delicate micro-electronics, our electric products are becoming far more sensitive. Computers, microwaves, stoves, washing machines and any product with a touch pad is especially vulnerable to power variations.

Most whole-house surge suppressors are connected to the inside electric power. If a surge hits, the surge protector takes the hit and sacrifices itself.

Power surges can also come down phone and cable TV lines. For this reason all three types of lines that bring power into your house, electric, telephone and cable lines, should be protected with surge protectors.

Unfortunately we can create our own power surges within the house just by turning pieces of equipment on and off that use large amounts of power. For this reason individual pieces of expensive electronic equipment, should be protected with specialized surge protection devices.

76 Don't rely on the power company to supply the electricity you need

On August 14, 2003 the electric power grid went down for about 1/3 of the country. This is not a one-time occurrence. We are going to be stuck with weather and demand related no power and low power occurrences for the rest of this century.

The question is whether you want to leave yourself hanging in the wind hoping your power company will work things out, or be pro-active and do something about it.

As Do-It-Yourselfers you have the power to literally take the power in your hands and provide your own power supply.

Many people will think that I am now going to start preaching that we should all attach solar collectors to our roofs and live off the energy the sun provides free of charge.

That's a great idea and I will be the first to sign up when I think it is practical. Unfortunately the technology is not there yet to collect solar energy and convert it to useable electric energy on a safe, cost effective basis.

The best way to assure your electric supply at the present time is with a power generator. Gasoline powered generators are only good as long as the fuel lasts. Multi-fuel generators, such as those sold around the world by Discount Compressor and Generator Co. of Pontiac are better because if you can't find one type of fuel, you may be able to find a supply of another.

Whole house natural gas powered generators are permanently connected to your electric system and, if you buy a big enough unit, can supply all your energy needs. The cost of whole house natural gas powered electric generators has gone way down. Many major companies are installing 10,000-watt generators for less than $7,000. If you have the need and the money, that's a bargain.

Photo courtesy of Coleman Powermante, Inc.

The size generator you buy, depends upon the power you and your family need to function. I've included a short table of the wattage that various appliances require for your use in analyzing your energy needs. You'll find a more comprehensive list on Discount Compressor's web site, www.gohonda.com. Keep in mind that an appliance may take up to three times the wattage when it starts.

Appliance energy requirements

Here is the number of watts it takes to run the following appliances

Appliance	Power requirement In watts
Radio	50
Color TV	300
Clothes dryer (gas)	400
Dishwasher	400
Computer	400
Furnace fan (1/3 hp)	1,200
Refrigerator/ freezer	600
Coffee maker	850
Microwave oven	800
Water heater (electric)	300
Well pump (1/3hp)	750
10,000 BTU air conditioner	1,500
Toaster	1,150
Electric oven	4,000
Hot tub	1,700
Space heater	1,200

Chapter VI
Emergencies

77 Things you need to have on hand in case of an emergency

Let's be honest. We all like to spend our lives as if we lived in the best of all possible worlds. We don't. September 11th proved that there are bad guys out there who want to do us ill. Mother nature shows us several times a year that she can shut down the roads, schools, power companies at will.

Greedy CEOs and CFOs prove that they have no concept of long term planning or the responsibility of public trust. Our governments (local, regional and national) prove that they can make legislation but have no walking around sense and hold no one at fault when the public trust is faulted.

Like it or not we are all out there, hanging by a thread, hoping that bad things won't happen. It just makes sense to spend a little time, money and energy right now to make sure that if something bad happens and you don't have the bare necessities for a week or two, you won't be caught short.

Start by playing your own war game and tallying up what you would need if the grocery and drug stores were out of inventory for two weeks. Businesses run on a "just-in-time" basis to save money. If the pipeline runs dry, supermarkets and drug stores have virtually no reserves.

If you figured out the amount of canned goods and other non-perishables your family would need to "get by" for those two weeks, then bought and stored everything on the list, you would have the necessities if disaster struck. Be sure to include a good first-aid kit.

Fuel storage facilities have to be refilled constantly. If your car runs out of gas, it is just a hunk of junk. Bicycles do not need gasoline and get you from here to there faster than feet. Having a bicycle in the garage for exercise would also give emergency transportation.

What about water? I think you should have at least a case or two of bottled water for everyone who lives in your house. If you live alone but the grandkids visit often, include a case of water for each of them. Bottled water can last for years.

Installing a reverse osmosis filter under the kitchen sink assures filtered water for cooking and drinking as long as there is water pressure. In today's age, this should be considered a necessary protection against premeditated terrorists and the "accidental terrorists" in government and industry responsible for ground spills and pollution.

As far as air quality is concerned, I have often advocated whole-house HEPA filtration systems for people with asthma or other bronchial conditions. A HEPA filter cannot protect you from a gas attack, but it can make your home's air cleaner and healthier than average. If you were unfortunate enough to live downwind of an occurrence such as the Twin Towers attack, it could make breathing easier. For more information, call Amaircare about their HEPA Bypass Filter or Broan-Nutone about their Guardian System.

In the event of an actual gas attack, some experts speculate that sealing the house and filtering all incoming air with a minimum of a MERV 8 filter and UV lights would keep the majority of the population safe.

Finally, we should all be prepared to live for a couple weeks without electricity. It only takes an ice storm to cut off the electricity and, if the "experts" are to be believed, a couple of falling trees can knock out the power grid.

Natural gas-powered electric generators are a good solution as long as natural gas supplies are maintained. Backup generators are expensive, but we are so dependent on electricity that anyone living in the northern tier of states or anyone that needs electricity to run medical equipment should consider one.

Every house needs an emergency light and a supply of flashlights, portable radios and extra batteries. If the batteries run out, one of the kinetic energy flashlights that you just shake to create about five minutes of light would be priceless. One of my listeners wrote to tell me that he and his wife existed very nicely by bringing in the solar powered landscape lighting and using it to light their house during the night.

I'd also recommend one of the crank back up portable radios advertised in the C. Crane catalog and Sharper Image stores.

You probably noticed that most of the things in this tip are not doomsday items. Most can be used in everyday life. Canned salmon or baked beans are great for lunch or a light dinner. It's fun to ride a bike. We all use bottled water. A crank-operated radio is a gas at the beach. Putting a little extra aside to use on a rainy day isn't weird it just makes sense.

78   Have an escape plan

We all know that we have to have smoke detectors and carbon monoxide detectors. Hopefully you have instigated a program where you change out their batteries twice a year when you change the clocks for daylight savings or regular time.

But what do you and the rest of the family do when the darned things go off in the middle of the night. Or what happens if someone is cooking and suddenly yells "fire"?

You have to have a plan that includes an escape route from the family room, kitchen and bedrooms. Someone has to be in charge of getting the cat, dog, bird, goldfish, gerbil or whatever other pets you have made members of your family.

Not only do you need a plan you need to practice it. If Junior is supposed to climb out of his bedroom window to get out of the house in the middle of the night, he better have the strength to open the window and be able to take out the screen and the ability to climb to safety. He should also be able to do all this literally in his sleep because that is when bad things are likely to happen.

A 2 a.m. fire drill may not make you popular, but it could save the lives of everyone who lives in the house.

You also need a designated assembly point. Some place close and easy to see yet far enough away from the house if there is a problem. The big tree in the neighbor's front yard might be a good choice. That way, in the event of a fire, you can count noses instantly and make certain that every one is out of harm's way.

Even if a fire should happen when we are gone for the day, we still have to worry about the dogs, cats, birds and other pets we leave behind.

The only way that a fireman can know that your house has pets is if you leave a prominently posted note by all the doors saying that there is a dog, cat, bird, etc. inside. If you have the animal caged (and that is a terrible thing to do to an animal for any length of time), the note has to tell where the animal is caged.

If Fireman Fred knows that your beagle Bozo is caged in the back bedroom, he will make every effort to go there and get him out. If he doesn't know your pet does not have a chance.

Planning now can keep your loved ones safe in an emergency.

79 Make certain every-one knows how to turn off the water and electricity

This may sound like a ridiculously simple tip but many people, especially children, do not know how to shut off the water and the electricity in an emergency. If a water pipe breaks or an electric switch or outlet has to be repaired this could turn into a read problem.

Water shutoff

The main water cut off valve is located right where the water supply line comes into the house. If you have a basement the line usually comes through the basement wall. If the house is on a slab or crawlspace the water line will often enter through the utility room wall.

If you are doing some plumbing work you can usually just turn off the water at the appliance. Hot and cold water supply lines are usually located under, over or beside each appli-ance. If you are working

Photos by Patrick Sheehan

on a sink, washing machine or dishwasher that uses both hot and cold water, be sure to turn off both valves.

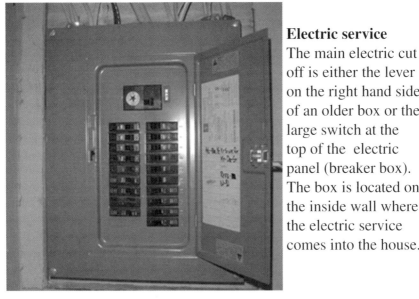

Electric service
The main electric cut off is either the lever on the right hand side of an older box or the large switch at the top of the electric panel (breaker box). The box is located on the inside wall where the electric service comes into the house.

If you have a basement it will be in the basement.

To shut off all the electricity in the house just pull down the lever. The one problem with this is that you may have to make the required electric repair with the aid of a flashlight and will have to reset all the electric clocks and timers in the house.

To make things more convenient you can open the panel and turn off the power supply to each individual circuit. This makes doing the repair a lot easier. The only problem is that you have to find the correct circuit or you will find doing the repair a shocking experience.

If you are doing a lot of electrical repairs, Zircon makes a special tool just to identify the circuit you need. The tool is called the CF12 Pro Circuit Breaker Finder.

80 Speed clean and sanitize a flooded basement

Perfectly clear ground water becomes polluted within 72-hours. The sooner the water is out of the basement the easier it will be to clean. If you still have a little standing water pump it out then vacuum up the residue with a Wet/Dry Shop Vac. Make certain the power plug is grounded, and wear rubber boots or rubber shoes.

Take out throw rugs or removable carpeting. Professional cleaning and sanitizing is best. If you can't send them out, clean the carpeting with a heavy-duty carpet cleaner.

Cut out wet drywall from finished basements

If you have a finished basement and water has gotten behind paneling or been wicked up into drywall or insulation, the infected areas have to be cut out and thrown away. Studs and concrete block or poured walls have to be sanitized and air dried for a prolonged period.

The entire area should be mopped with a mixture of germicide and water. Nothing I know of is better or cheaper than 3/4-cup of household bleach in 5 gallons of water. That is a strong chemical solution so be sure to wear a respirator.

My friends in the janitorial supply business tell me that if you fear fecal or other organic contamination, it is best to sanitize with a microbial such as Push by Betco or Enzym D by Big D Industries. These products contain living, nonpathogenic microorganisms that consume any organic matter that may be on the floor or in the carpeting. Mix approximately a half-gallon to 5 gallons of water and apply with an extractor. If the carpeting is just wet, they recommend Betco Cleanitizer to clean and decontaminate the carpet.

Dry out the basement immediately
Get air circulating immediately to dry wall-to-wall carpeting. If you have a dehumidifier, put it at one end of the room and place an oscillating fan at the other. Hook up the oscillating fan to an appliance timer. Six hours on, two hours off, for a total of 18 hours out of 24. Tilt the fan toward the basement ceiling.

Padding, under very wet wall-to-wall carpeting may have to be replaced. In a worst case scenario, the carpeting may have to be thrown out, too. Upholstered furniture that has been contaminated also has to go.

Left damp mold will grow everywhere in the basment. This shot shows mold on concrete walls, duct work, wood support and ceiling. Photo courtesy of Sanit-Air

Don't sacrifice your health for your bank account
If this sounds like a lot of work you're right. There is a good chance the work involved may be past your physical endurance. Don't sacrifice your health for your bank account. Many carpeting and remediation companies have special water remediation services. The problem is that time is critical and half the local population will be trying to get their services the same time you are.

Let your fingers do the walking before you have a problem. Ask for recommendations. See if your carpet cleaner provides this service. Check the Yellow Pages. Professionals have the kind of heavy-duty fans and super dehumidifiers that we can only dream about.

As soon as you find people who sound like they do good work, put their names and phone numbers in your personal phone book. If you have a basement flooding event, call these people and schedule an appointment for as soon as the rain or flooding stops. Being first on their list can be the difference between the job being an annoying inconvenience and a health and bank account catastrophe.

Find out what went wrong
When the muscle work is over, put your brain in gear. Track down why the flooding happened and what you can do to prevent similar problems in the future.

Many people with sunken window wells have flooded basements. Good window well drainage is critical. Debris has to be cleaned out at least every spring and late fall. Some window wells have drains. The drains must be clear or they compound the problem.

The natural drainage in most sunken window wells is composed of various strata of gravel, topped by construction sand. Weathering leaks silt on top of the sand, and clogs the gravel. Dig out and replace the clogged sand and gravel.

Consider replacing the sunken windows with glass block. You will still have to keep the window wells clear, but the block will give you better protection against flooding.

Storm sewers should not back up into the basement, but they do. If this happens more than once, have the line from your main drain to the street snaked out periodically. The bigger the trees near your house, the more often it will have to be done.

If your sump pump shut off at a critical time, check to see why. When the electric power goes out, the electric sump pump stops working. This usually means that the sump pump is inoperative when the need is greatest. Consider installing a sump pump that runs on city water pressure, not electricity.

81 What to do if the roof leaks

Leaking roofs can be tricky; you may not even know it is happening until major damage has been done. If you are out of town and no one is checking on your home while you are away, the floors, walls and ceilings may be ruined before anyone even knows about it.

Winter can be especially dangerous
During the winter the roof may be leaking and you may not even know about it. The only way to find out is to go up into the attic. Turn on all the lights and bring a very strong flashlight. Inspect the attic thoroughly. If the nails in the roof deck are rusty or wet it means there is a moisture problem.

The water may not have been caused by a roof dam or shingle damage. It may not even be coming from the outside. Many houses have so much hot air leaking into the attic from below that sufficient water condenses on the underside of the roof deck to cause water damage.

If the attic ceiling is OK, get on your hands and knees and check the insulation in the soffit area. Wet or damp insulation means that water is coming in from the outside. It may be leaking down into the walls or the ceilings of the house.

You must discover the water trail
Try to discover the water trail. Water can drain into the ceiling or walls and travel along wood or wiring to other parts of the house. It can actually flow in a horizontal plane.

If you discover major water damage call your homeowner insurance agent immediately. You may also want to call a remediation specialist.

If you can find it get a thermographic scan
If you cannot follow the path of the water, call a company like Monroe Infrared Technologies or Midwest Infrared. Get them to do an infrared scan of the house while the area is still wet. Before drying, the water will show as an easily identifiable line that you can follow from initial entry point to final destination. The infrared scan will also be immensely valuable dealing with insurance adjusters because it shows the full extent of the water damage and leaves no room for guesswork.

Dry out the attic
Do everything possible to dry out the attic. Rake up and discard wet, loose fiberglass or cellulose insulation. Wet attic fiberglass batt insulation can be dried and re-used, according to Owens Corning. Everything else must be thrown away.

Dry heat is needed. Turn up the furnace thermostat to 78 degrees Fahrenheit. Turn off the humidistat. Bring fans up to the attic. Connect the fans to outdoor extension cords and keep them running continuously.

If water has gotten into electric receptacles, turn off the power to the outlets and drain the fixtures.

Every wet area inside the house must be opened up and dried thoroughly, according to Connie Morbach of Sanit-Air. Connie and her husband Tom Morbach have a leading air quality testing and remediation company.

"If you have water damage in a wall or ceiling, the first thing to do is drain the area. Then remove any wet insulation. If there is just a small amount of water damage to plaster or wood you may be able to just let it dry. If the damage covers a wide area, or the affected

surface is drywall, it must be cut out and replaced," Morbach says.

Time critical

"Time is critical. If you can open up the wall or ceiling, remove wet insulation and start drying the area with fans within 48 hours there is little health risk.

If an area has been wet for three days or more, never attempt to dry it with fans. After 72 hours only commercial dehumidifiers should be used safely. Blowing fans will spread contamination throughout the house.

"The reason for the time limit is that after 72 hours the bacteria count in drywall that has been soaked with clean roof water is as high as that of drywall soaked a day in sewer water. If the molds are allowed to develop, the family could have major health problems and the entire area may have to be torn out and sanitized," surface is drywall, it must be cut out and replaced." Morbach says.

Even water draining down the outside of a house can cause major problems. Melting water can get into older fabric-covered cables and drain into wall-mounted breaker boxes. If you see water coming out of the breaker box, call a licensed electrician immediately. There is nothing you can do to stop water from draining down and flooding breaker boxes. It is only a matter of time before the box blows and there is a major possibility of fire damage or personal injury so get help immediately.

82 Black mold panic

Mold has been in the news a great deal over the past few years. The size and number of homeowners' mold claims have lead to a revolution in the insurance industry so that now many insurers do not provide coverage for mold damage claims. Or, if they do provide coverage it is for a very limited amount for a relatively high premium.

Is this likely to become a problem for you or is this just something that happens to other people?

According to "Biological Pollutants in Your Home," (EPA Document reference # 402-F-90-102) a brochure prepared by the American Lung Association and the U.S. consumer Products Commission "one third to one half of all structures have damp conditions that may encourage development of pollutants such as molds and bacteria, which can cause allergic reactions - including asthma and spread infectious diseases."

The key phrase is "one third to one half of all structures." In other words if your house doesn't have a mold problem, the neighbor's house to the right of you or the left of you probably does.

Put another way, if you have two grown children and they each have homes of their own, if your house doesn't have a mold problem, one of theirs probably does.

I happen to have two grown children. Each has a home of their own. That makes the problem pretty up close and personal.

Mold is not something rare. Mold is all over. It is absolutely essential to life because it breaks down organic mater and permits it to be recycled. Yeasts that permit us to bake bread or make beer and cheese are in the fungi family. Fungi are just another name for mold and mildew.

Molds are highly adaptable organisms. They can be single cells, like yeast, or strings of cells called hyphae. Hyphae weave themselves into clusters, called mycelium that are visible to the naked eye.

Mold spores germinate to form hyphae, which grow into a colony and create more spores. If the climate is good the cycle goes on forever and the mold colony spreads and prospers. If the climate turns bad the fungi form thick walled chlamy-dospores which can survive for years in hot dry climates and start the life cycle all over again

Mold covered stove top and cabinet. Photo courtesy of Health Chek, LLC (c) 2003

when proper climatic conditions return.

According to a very excellent publication by the Foundation of the Wall and Ceiling Industry, 69,000 different species of fungi have been identified and there may be as many as 1,500,000 different species.

All told, fungi (remember that is just another name for mold) represent approximately 25 percent of the Earth's biomass. The publication, "Mold: Cause, Effect and Response," is available to download free on the foundation's web site: www.awci.org. OK, molds are all over, but most molds are benign and we don't have to worry about them. There are just a few bad apples, like Stachybotrys, that we have to worry about. Right?

All molds can be harmful

According to the Environmental Protection Agency, "All molds have the potential to cause long term health effects. Molds produce allergens, irritants, and in some cases, toxins that may cause reaction in humans." (Quoted from "Mold Remediation in Schools and Commercial Buildings," EPA # 402-K-01-001).

Potential mold dangers can be created by the living mold, by the mycotoxins (toxic substances) they produce, and even from dead mold cells.

Despite the potential danger very little practical research has been done on mold danger in houses. We know that there are some extremely poisonous mycotoxins, like Aflatoxin B that can be produced by Aspergillus flavus and Aspergillus parasiticus. But these molds are found on contaminated grains, not buildings.

Stachybotrys and alternaria Aspergillus and Ulocladium mold growing on drywall in mold cavaty. photo courtesy of Health Chek, LLC (c) 2003

Most of the research has been concerned with molds and myc-otoxins that are eaten, not aspirated (breathed in). Most of the newspaper and TV coverage about mold problems has centered on Stachybotrys. That is not the only mold that can cause problems.

I have included a mold chart in the Appendix that summarizes much of the information about many of the problem indoor molds. I do not want to frighten you but I do want you to know the extent of the problem you may have to confront one day.

83 What this means to you

I get letters and e-mails from thousands of people. My heart goes out to many of them but unfortunately I do not have the time, money or staff to reply to most. My staff and I do what we can by writing a weekly Question and Answer column that runs in the Detroit News and is distributed by the Gannett News Service.

I would like you to read one of the many e-mails I have received on mold and the injuries that are becoming fairly common place in many North American communities. Naturally I am not using the writers true name.

"Dear Glenn: I am a victim of black mold. We bought a house in December of 2000. When we bought our house the owners lied on the disclosure statement about water damage and mold. Our inspector did not do a good job and missed what I consider obvious water damage in the basement.

"To make a very long story short. By the time we knew the extent of the damage and what we were dealing with (Stachybotrys), we had already lived in the house for 7 months.

"My youngest son lost his hair and his already bad asthma was aggravated. My older son developed severe mold allergies and his asthma became acute. My husband went through 2 spells of pneumonia. I had nose bleeds, developed severe asthma, I still have neurological damage (numbness, twitching, severe cramping in the hands and feet, fatigue and spells of memory loss).

"The doctors think I have mycotoxicosis (Poisoning caused by ingestion of a mycotoxin.). I have no idea about cancer and the risks my family may now have to face.

"We have lost everything we own. The cost to remediate the home to an empty shell is around $60,000. We would then have to refinish it and replace all that we own.

"We have just walked away. Our mortgage company is threatening to sue. Our family has moved in with my parents and commutes over an hour to work. My children share a twin bed or sleep on the floor. We had to find a new home for our family dog because there was no place for him at my folks.

"Mold is a real threat to your health and your livelihood. I have often wished we had suffered a house fire or flood. Then at least our insurance would have covered something and there are agencies in place to help those kinds of victims.

"Our insurance company would not cover our loss, even though we have mold coverage. Their reason for denial of the claim was that condition was preexisting.

"I am glad to see the coverage in the paper. I have written the newspapers on many occasions looking for coverage and help and I put the same effort toward the TV news. It appears that my family's situation is old news.

"I have rambled on too long but just wanted you to know that there are many like me and we appreciate the coverage.

Sincerely,
Julia M."

That's what you have to worry about.

Julia said it far better than I. The big headlines and jury awards are long gone. The insurance industry has sidestepped coverage. Thousands of homeowners, people just like you and me, are losing their shirts or ignoring the problem and living in conditions that may ruin their health.

To date almost every executive I know in the mold testing and remediation business has developed severe mold sensitivity and gets physically sick any time they enter a mold-infested building without a mask. Julia's letter shows that people who live in sick buildings get just as sick.

I do not want this to happen to you or your loved ones.

This problem is 100 % related to water infiltration and damage. It disappears if you keep your house dry.

Please do everything you can to protect your house from water damage. If something happens don't procrastinate. Don't wait for the problem to go away or for an insurance company or builder to fix it for you. Fix it right away. Your health is more important than your pocket book.

Even if you hope for help from an insurance company timely action to limit damage is required in every insurance policy.

84 Mold remediation

If you have a mold problem and the total cumulative area does not exceed 10 square feet you can probably take care of it yourself. Over 10 square feet you really need a professional. If the problem is under 10 square feet and it comes back again after you have tried to solve the problem yourself, you need a professional.

If you smell mold but can't find the problem you need to have an air testing company make a physical inspection of your house to find the mold source and check the air quality. If you want a preliminary mold test, Health Chek, LLC, (866) 234-7579, www.moldchek.net, has a very inexpensive Mold Chek Sampling Kit. There is an additional charge for analyzing the kit once you have collected the sample.

Most of the air quality testing organizations I know have gotten out of the mail order test kit business because they find that an on premises inspection and professional sample collection is vital to doing a thorough analysis of a location. I agree with them.

Be warned. A mold inspection is quite often not a pretty thing. To do his or her job properly the inspector must have your permission to remove fixtures and knock holes in plaster drywall if they believe the problem may be lurking behind the surface, under wallpaper or in the wall cavity. Long-term mold problems are seldom confined to one tidy area. Water intrusion can begin in one area and flow to the other side of the house creating several problem mold areas.

Find the leak and fix it
Mold is caused by a water problem. It is estimated that three-quarters of the time the source of that water is a leaky pipe or fixture. One fourth of the time the problem is a leak in the building envelope. This could mean anything from water coming in through the roof or condensation in the attic to water coming in through leaky window flashings, loose siding or a basement water problem.

Whatever the problem you have to find the source and fix it before remediation can begin.

I am going to give you some of the basic principals of mold remediation and give you step-by-step instructions on how to clean up a very small mold area. I have based most of my recommendations on the more liberal Canadian mold remediation suggestions.

Basic tools
When we think of mold remediation we think of people in moon suits that make them look like astronauts doing who knows what in a vacated building.

In its earliest and most benign form you can get by with soap and water. All the literature suggests a non-perfumed detergent so that mold smell is not masked and you can tell if you have cleared the area.

If you want to use a product specifically made to kill mold and mildew, consider Amazon Products Mildew Stain Away. It is much easier on the lungs than a bleach and water solution. Should you want to sterilize the area with a bleach and water solution, a 10 to one solution (1 part household bleach to 10 parts water) is considered adequate.

Small area (less than 10 square feet)
If you are clearing a small area you should wear goggles, rubber gloves and a disposable dust mask such as the 3M 8210 at a minimum. Personally I would prefer that you were wearing a respirator.

Washable surfaces should be scrubbed with an unscented detergent solution, then sponged clean with a wet rag.

According to Canadian specifications moldy drywall with just a tiny bit of mold that has not penetrated the surface can be cleaned with a damp rag using baking soda or a bit of detergent. If the drywall gets soaked it has to be cut out and replaced.

Moderate Area (cumulatively less than a 4 x 8 piece of plywood) As far as I am concerned if you have this much mold you probably have more that you have not discovered and the matter should be turned over to professional remediators.

If you have to try and get rid of the mold yourself you have to upgrade your precautions and tools considerably.

The family should be out of the house while work is going on. The work area should be isolated with plastic sheeting.

A HEPA filter vacuum cleaner is necessary. Do not use a vacuum cleaner that does not have a HEPA filter.

You should wear a respirator, rubber gloves and goggles.

Vacuum effected and surrounded surfaces with a HEPA filter vacuum cleaner. Scrub or brush surfaces with a mild detergent and water solution, then sponge clean with a wet rag. Repeat twice then dry quickly.

Wooden surfaces
Wood should be cleaned as outlined. If you can't get the mold out of the wood, sand lightly with a vacuum sander such as the Sand & Kleen by Magna Industries.

Concrete surfaces
Concrete should be vacuumed and washed down with the detergent solution. If the area still is mold stained wash down the area with a solution of one cup dry measure of TSP (Trisodium Phosphate) dissolved in two gallons of water. Stir the solution to make certain that the TSP is completely dissolved. Keep area to be cleaned damp with the TSP solution for 15 minutes before rinsing twice with clear water. Dry thoroughly.

Drywall
Your best bet is to tear out and discard the effected drywall. Wash down the wall cavity and dry thoroughly. Do not replace the drywall until the reason for the mold has been solved, the area thoroughly dry and the air quality has been checked and proven to be mold free.

Carpeting
Moldy carpeting and padding should be
 thrown away. Do not replace until you know the area is totally dry and mold free. If I had my druthers I would let the area go uncarpeted for a couple of months so that I knew the area was totally dry and the problem would not return.

Large Areas

Anything over 30 square feet must be remediated by professionals and overseen by a health and safety professional with experience performing microbial investigations.

You and I are not qualified to even attempt this kind of work. The remediation must be performed by personnel trained in the handling of hazardous materials and equipped with cartridge respirators, gloves and goggles.

The entire area is sealed off with plastic sheeting before work begins. If the work is going to be dusty or the area is larger than 100 square feet (that is only 10 feet x 10 feet) work should be done in compliance with New York City Level IV Decontamination Guidelines.

This shot shows painted drywall on walls and ceiling covered with Cladosporium, Aspergillus and Penicillium molds. Photo courtesy of Health Chek, LLC

In this case the area is completely sealed off from the rest of the house with plastic sheeting and an exhaust fan with a HEPA filter is used to generate negative pressure. Airlocks and a decontamination room are installed.

Under Level IV conditions workers have to be protected with full-face respirators with high efficiency particulate air (HEPA) cartridges, disposable protective clothing covering both head and shoes, and gloves.

Mold areas have to be completely eliminated. Contaminated materials that cannot be cleaned such as drywall and carpeting must be removed in sealed plastic bags. Contaminated wood, is often cut out and replaced. Sometimes structural wood can be saved through use of soda blasting which grinds away the contaminated area leaving raw, uncontaminated wood.

The work area and adjoining area must be vacuumed with a HEPA vacuum and cleaned with a damp cloth or mop and a detergent solution. All areas must be dry and visibly free from contamination and debris before the job is finished.

Naturally the area has to be vacated until work is completed and the area declared free from contamination. This can easily stretch into a several week period so make provisions for a comfortable place to stay.

Detailed information - free for the asking
You can get far better and more detailed information on the web. I would like to especially recommend four publications.

"Mold Remediation in Schools and Commercial Buildings" by the U.S. Environmental Protection Agency. You can download this 48-page document from the EPA web site: http://www.epa.gov/iaq/molds/moldguide.html. The publication should also be available in printed form. For more information consult the EPA Indoor Air Quality Information Clearinghouse, (800) 438-4318.

This detailed guide gives information on how to inspect for mold, probable sources, and step-by-step remediation techniques. It shows photographs of mold infected areas, protective gear, etc.

"Fighting Mold – The homeowners' Guide" by Canada Mortgage

& Housing Corporation (CMHC). Go to the CMHC web site www.cmhc-schl.gc.ca/en/index.cfm, then click on Building, renovating & maintaining >Self-Help and Problem Solving >Humidity >Moisture and Mold.

This is a short 8-page, easy to read document that is very hands on and tells you how to clean up small, medium and large mold problems on a house by house basis. It says that most homeowners can even clean up a "moderate" size mold contamination by themselves if they take proper precautions.

"Mold: Cause, Effect and Response" by the Foundation of the Wall and Ceiling Industry (FWCI). This 44-page brochure gives an excellent summary of the problem, many of the different types of mold, mold remediation techniques and tips on finding a good mold remediation contractor. You can download the document from the FWCI's web site: www.awci.org.

Three of the best pieces of advice in the brochure are: "Get a professional." "Don't go cheap." "You get what you pay for." That advice goes double for a homeowner who learns that he or she is living in a mold infected house.

"Guidelines on Assessment and Remediation of Fungi in Indoor Environments" by the New York City Department of Health & Mental Hygiene Bureau of Environmental & Occupational Disease Epidemiology, updated January 2002.

This is the famous New York City Guidelines. It lists the criteria and generally accepted practices upon which almost all mold remediation is based. If a mold remediation company says that they work according to New York Guidelines, this is it. You can find it on the web at: *www.ci.nyc.ny.us/html/doh/html/epi/moldrpt1.html.*

If you have trouble getting to this page, go to Google and do a search for *"Guidelines on Assessment and Remediation of Fungi in Indoor Environments".*

85 Don't get sandbagged by your insurance company

When the homeowners policy of my editor at Master Handyman Press came up for renewal we got an entire range of quotes just to compare prices for the same coverage from different insurance companies. Prices ranged from $956 to $2,589 a year.

It turned out that the price differential was just the tip of the iceberg. Rick Sovel, a certified and licensed insurance counselor and partner in the Michigan Community Insurance Agency told us that depending on the wording, the actual coverage on a claim could vary a $100,000 or more. It could even determine whether there is coverage.

By now most homeowners known that their homeowner's policy contains little or no coverage for mold damage. Some home insurers have even done everything possible to limit any and all water damage claims. A number of insurance companies have even decided to opt out of the homeowners insurance business in states that have been hard hit by mold and water damage claims. Some insurance companies have set policies that automatically refuse to renew homeowners who have had as few as three previous claims.

With all this happening it is very important to understand exactly what is and what is not covered by your insurance policy. Choosing one company over the other because of a $100 difference in the annual premium could be foolhardy and even submitting a petty insurance claim could cause your policy not t be renewed.

Here are a few of the other policy provisions you should discuss with your insurance agent.

Different types of homeowners insurance

It is very difficult for the average person to be able to read a policy and know what it means. For example, "broad form" sounds like it gives a lot of coverage. Actually "special coverage" gives broader protection.

Ordinance and law coverage

"Ordinance and law" is an option, which only costs $20 to $50 per year but could decide whether you can afford to rebuild in the event of a catastrophic loss. "Let's say you have a very nice older house that was built in 1960 and insured for $300,000. A fire destroys 80 percent of the house. Since 80 percent of the house has been destroyed, the insurance company would write you a check for 80 percent of the total," Sovel says.

"Many municipal ordinances state that where only 20 percent of a house remains, the entire house must be demolished. Unless they have ordinance and law coverage, the home owner has to pay for demolishing, removing and rebuilding the remaining 20 percent," Sovel says. Additionally, most homeowners' policies only require the insurer to bring the building up to its original condition. Without ordinance and law coverage, the homeowner will be required to pay the difference between old and new building code requirements.

Guaranteed replacement cost

Many policies used to have a guaranteed replacement benefit, which said that if it cost more than the policy limit to rebuild a structure, the insurance company would pay the additional cost subject to other policy provisions. This led a number of people to under-insure their houses. The insurance companies' response has been to change the name and limit the coverage. Depending on the insurance company, 'extended dwelling coverage' limits the percentage the insurer will pay over and above the face amount of the policy from 15 percent to 25 percent.

Finished basements at risk

"Many insurance companies will not provide coverage for sump pump problems or sewer and drain back up, and severely limit coverage on finished basements. If you have a finished basement, are considering finishing the basement or even use it to store valuables, make certain your homeowners policy provides coverage in the event of a loss," Sovel says.

Policy limits

There is no correlation between the market value of a house and its replacement cost. Market value projects what you could buy a similar house for today. Replacement cost reflects the cost of tearing down and rebuilding the dwelling. Most of us live in subdivisions built by builders who constructed several homes at a time. The homebuyer benefits from economies of scale on architectural plans, building materials and construction crew efficiencies.

If you moved into a brand-new $400,000 house today, it would cost a good deal more to rebuild the house next week. In the event of a total loss, debris would have to be carried away, the architect must draw up plans to rebuild the house according to the existing footprint, and materials and crews have to be specially scheduled.

Extended umbrella coverage

It is very easy for coverage to fall between the cracks. A million dollar, or even a multi-million dollar umbrella policy that provides coverage for normally uninsured risks or liabilities usually costs very little extra and can provide a great deal of peace of mind.

Ask your insurance agent about these policy provisions and about the possibility of adding mold damage and finished basement coverage to your present policy. Also, get him to tell you about the cancellation policy of your insurer. If you don't get answers, or like the answers you get, start shopping for a new policy maybe even a new agent.

86 Remember the remediation company works for you not the insurance company

Since "into every life a little rain must fall" it is highly probable that sooner or later something is going to happen to your house and you will be calling for an insurance repair.

The claim adjuster will probably offer suggestions for one or more remediation contractors. That's wonderful. You probably do not have any remediation contractors on your Christmas card list and therefore do not know who is any good or who knows your insurance company's claims procedures. Working with someone who already knows the way and does not have to use the trial and error method is very helpful.

Unfortunately that same remediation contractor also knows your insurance company's way for doing things (cheap), and may have already fought and lost the good fight so many times that they now take the path of least resistance.

Don't accept the insurance company's recommendation for a remediation contractor blindly. Interview them. Get them to pitch you on how they will do the job. Look for quality assurances and ask for references.

Remember, the insurance company is going to give you money and the remediation contractor works for you. He or she has to please you. Pleasing you may take going to the mat with the insurance company. It may take money over and above the settlement of the insurance claim.

You have already had a lot of stress. At the end of the day you want a remediation company that will do a quality job and make the project as hassle free as possible.

87 Make certain you are not an easy target

"The price of freedom is eternal vigilance." It is also the cost of successful home ownership. For most of us our homes are not only our biggest single investment, but probably pays us the biggest rate of return.

Our homes cannot take care of themselves. If we want them to reach their full investment and comfort potential we have to constantly maintain and upgrade them.

In 2001 we Americans spent $214 billion on home improvements. That was more money than commercial and public works construction, legal services and clothing store sales. Any target that big and tempting is bound to have a fair number of ne'er-do-wells looking for a quick score. They will only be successful with you if you fail to follow the fundamentals I have outlined in this book.

Do not choose a contractor because he or she has a nice smile or is good to your dog. Demand and check references. Read and upgrade contracts. Demand completion dates. Don't pay too much down. Don't be greedy. If a price is too good you are being sucked into a scam or dealing with someone who does not know what they are doing. Either way you are going to wind up a looser.

Learn all you can before you do, find a good contractor or do it yourself, then brag about the result.

Chapter VII

Maintenance

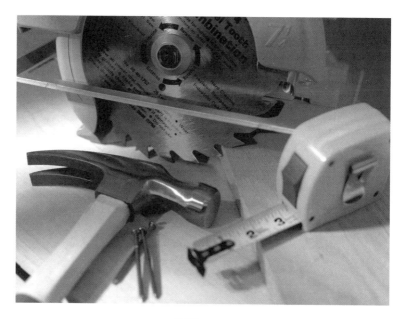

88 How to inspect your home's exterior

It's a good idea to inspect the exterior of your house every spring and fall. In the spring you need to see the damage perpetrated by Old Man Winter. In the fall you need to see what last minute chores need to be done to get your home ready for the long, cold months ahead.

Grab a pencil and pad of paper and walk around the outside of your house three times and make out your to-do list.

First trip: Roof and gutters

I usually do this chore with a pair of binoculars. You may have to go into your neighbor's yard to get the proper perspective. Look for worn, damaged or curling shingles. Check to see that there are

no cracks in the valleys created by rooflines coming together. Check the flashing around the chimney and roof vents. Look for sagging gutters.

If anything has deteriorated, someone —preferably a roofing professional — will have to climb up on the roof. If the roofing cement around the flashing of the chimney is hard and beginning to separate, it should be removed and re-applied.

Second trip: Building perimeter

Walk close to the house, look up to the roof over-hang and count the number of soffit vents. One of every three soffit panels should be vented. If you can see daylight between the fascia board and gutter, the gutters are pulling away. If the fascia board has turned spongy it has to be replaced. If it is solid, upgrade the hanger system to gutter brackets with screws.

Carefully inspect the windows and siding for any sign of weathering or wood rot. Soft, rotting wood means that water is getting trapped. No matter how hard we try to prevent entry, water will penetrate the envelope of the house during a driving rain or freeze-and-thaw conditions. That water has to drain out of the house. Rotten wood is a sign that drainage is plugged. Track down and solve the problem.

Replace hardened caulk and window putty. If double-glazed windows are cloudy, the seal has broken and the glass, not the frame, should be replaced.

Check all openings where pipes and wires penetrate the house. Seal openings with flexible caulk so that water, insects and rodents cannot enter.

Third trip: Ground slope

Look at the ground, deck and outside equipment such as barbecues and lawn furniture.

The ground and even the concrete or asphalt drive or patio slab must drain away from the house. Ground should be graded so that the slope drops 1-inch per foot for approximately a 5 foot distance from the house.

If the slope has flattened or reversed, it is time to rebuild the slope.

When transplanting flowers or shrubs the ground often sinks and creates puddles I call birdbaths. These areas have to be filled with dirt, and then tamped down so that the puddle cannot reoccur.

If you have a deck, get a flashlight and check the slope of the ground underneath the deck. If the ground has started slanting toward the house, shovel enough sand under the house to reverse the slope. If you have a large deck, you may have to lift a few of the deck boards nearest the house so that you can get the sand where it belongs.

Concrete slabs sloping toward the house have to be mud jacked to reverse the slope. If the drive has cracked or the expansion strip between slopes has worn away you need to make repairs to prevent further damage.

Make certain that sunken window wells are free of debris and that gutter downspout drains extend at least five feet away from the house.

By now you should have a to-do list that will keep you busy. Don't get overwhelmed. Organize your list and do one job at a time, then brag about the result.

89   How to assure proper drainage and a dry basement

The majority of wet basements are caused not by cracks or defects but by exterior drainage. The building codes all call for land around the basement to slope away from the house one inch per foot.

That means that the ground five feet away from the basement will be five inches lower than the ground abutting the basement. This height differential insures that rain and melting snow drains away from, not toward, the house. This drainage puts the basement walls on a water free diet.

Over the years the ground banked up against the basement walls washes away. Flower planting and weeding accentuate the process and little by little the ground changes from draining away from to draining toward the house.

When you see this it is time to re-establish the slope. This is not just a matter of piling dirt up around the basement. The procedure is to remove the sod; make a 2-foot deep by 2-foot wide trench; then re-build.

This is a major job. After trenching, put in a bottom layer of 8 inches of pea gravel, followed by 8 inches of sand. Top off with 8 or more inches of topsoil and replace the sod. The final result should drain rainwater away from the house and help keep the basement dry.

90 How to reestablish drainage in a sunken window well

When the drainage from a sunken window is plugged water can build up in a well during a major storm. If that happens the pressure from the water will eventually break through a window pane and flood the basement.

The procedure for reestablishing drainage in a sunken window is identical to that of reestablishing the slope.

You have to climb down into the well and clean out all the leaves, branches and other clutter that has fallen into the well.
Then take an entrenching tool or other short handled shovel and dig down two feet.

Put in 8 inches of coarse gravel, 8 inches of fine gravel and 8 inches of topsoil.

91 Choose the right caulk and the job is easy

Caulking is a prime factor in protecting you and the rest of the family from cold winter drafts and it really cuts down on the heating bills. Loose mortar allows not only wind and cold, but also rain to get behind the brick surface. Gibraltar's new Mortar Mix in a caulk tube makes fixing the problem very easy. Left uncorrected, the problem can degenerate the entire brick wall and result in astronomical repair bills.

Caulking

GE recommends a "caulk walk" around the house inspecting everything that's mounted to your home or enters the house. That includes spigots, windows, doors, vents, TV and phone cables, air-conditioning lines, siding connections and the line where the siding meets the foundation as well as along side chimneys.

On the inside of the house you should caulk windows, doors, electrical outlets, counters and countertops, sinks, bathtubs, tub enclosures, around pipes, miscellaneous openings and plumbing.

Anywhere the old caulk has pulled away from the corners and the edges it is supposed to be sealing, or has lost resiliency needs to be replaced. Don't just look, give all the caulk lines you see the old thumb test. If it doesn't give a little when you push in then bounce back, remove it. Do not caulk over it.

Caulk selection

One of the easiest ways to get totally confused is to go to the caulk aisle at Home Depot, Lowes, Menards or any of the other big boxes. You see so many different types, brands and now colors of caulks your brain starts spinning and your eyes cross.

Believe it or not, this is a good thing. The huge variety lets you fine tune your purchase to fit your exact needs.

Caulks used to be like Model-T Fords, Fords came in any color you wanted as long as it was black. All caulks were white. Many would not accept paint so you were stuck with little white lines all over the place. Now caulks come in several different colors and most can be painted.

Silicone caulks adhere so well that you have a devil of a time cleaning them off. They are excellent for extreme conditions but cannot be painted and clean-up is with mineral spirits.

Water-based acrylic caulks can be painted and give soap and water clean-up.

Latex-based caulks can be painted and give soap and water clean-up.

Latex caulks with silicone try to combine the ease of latex with the strength of silicone.

Premium elastomeric caulks combine superior flexibility and durability of a silicone with excellent paintability and soap and water clean-up.

Many caulks are now mildew resistant, some are rated for both interior and exterior use, and some are just for interior. Some are made for wet environments like sinks, showers and bathtubs.

Some caulks are packaged for caulk guns. Some have squeeze tubes. Some come in easy-to-use aerosol cans. The last are excellent for first time Do-It-Yourselfers or folks who do not have strong hands because they give excellent control and all you have to do is push down on the tip for the caulk to be released.

If you take the time to study the caulk aisle you will find the exact caulk to fit your needs and skill.

While you are in the caulk aisle look for a caulk shaping tool. There are several different types. All give you the ability to smooth and shape the bead like a professional after the caulk is applied.

Caulk removal
Outside, the best way to remove old caulk is to soften it with a heat gun or Bernz-O-Matic Torch. The Bernz-O-Matic Torch is faster, but the heat gun is safer.

When the caulk gets pliable, scrape it away with a hooknose linoleum knife or a chisel point putty knife. Be sure to scrape away all the caulk. Leaving any residue will stop the new caulk from forming a water tight seal.

Inside the house you can use a caulk remover like those made by 3M or Dap. Caulk removers are made for Latex based caulk so if you are trying to remove a silicone you will only have limited success.

For Latex/Acrylic caulks clear away old caulk, wash down with a window cleaner and air dry.

For Silicone caulks, GE recommends that concrete, masonry & stone have all old sealant and dirt removed with a wire brush and all contaminants such as water repellents and surface treatments removed. Porous surfaces should be sanded. Metal, glass and plastic should be cleaned with solvents such as mineral spirits and alcohol, then wiped dry with a clean cloth or lintless paper toweling. Solvents should never be allowed to air dry without wiping.

Application

A good caulking gun and a gentle hand are key ingredients. Paying a little extra for your caulking gun will make a big difference in the quality of the job.

When you load the caulk cylinder cut the tip on a 45-degree angle, pierce the seal, then load it into the gun. Use either the push or pull method of application. In pushing you inject the bead in front of the gun. In pulling you reverse the gun and trail caulk after the gun.

Pushing applies caulk more deeply into the crevices. Pulling is often the only way rough surfaces can be caulked.

Whichever method you choose, apply as narrow a bead as possible because you can always apply more caulk, but removing surplus caulk can be a problem.

Remember any gap over 1/2 inch wide is an architectural gap and must be filled with backer rod before the caulk is applied.

92 How to caulk the bathtub so the job lasts and doesn't leak

Bathtubs are one of the hardest areas to caulk successfully. This is because an empty bathtub weighs hundreds of pounds less than a tub that is filled with water (especially when you are in the tub). This weight differential makes the tub flex stretching the caulk and breaking the seal of old dry caulk.

If caulking the tub is on your list here is the fast, easy way to get great results.

Shopping List: caulk remover, non-ammoniated household cleaner, household bleach, rubbing alcohol, your choice of tub & tile caulk with anti mildew additive, paper toweling, wood or plastic putty knife, old tooth brush or hand brush, goggles, rubber gloves, respirator, caulking gun (if required), caulk shaping tool.

Directions:
1. Fill tub 1/2-full of water. This pulls the edges of the bathtub away from the walls so that you can seal the tub when it has the most strain. You can also deep clean and sterilize the maximum space between the tub and walls.
2. Apply caulk remover around tub top, down sides and along the floor.
3. Wait 2-hours for remover to loosen caulk.
4. Remove caulk with a wood or plastic putty knife. Reapply caulk remover as necessary to loosen the remaining old caulk.
5. Clean the entire area with the non-ammoniated cleaner. Really get in the cracks with the bristles of the hand brush or toothbrush.

6. Carefully sterilize the area between the tub and walls and tub and floor with household bleach. This is strong stuff, open a window and put on a respirator. You want any traces of mold or mildew to be totally gone before you are done.
7. Wipe down with paper toweling.
8. Wipe down the area to be sealed with rubbing alcohol. The entire area has to be squeaky, antiseptically clean when you are finished. Rub your hand up and down the caulk lines. If you feel anything but smooth you have not finished cleaning.
9. Alcohol dries almost instantly but make sure that the tub sides, walls and floor are bone dry before you proceed to the next step.
10. Caulk the tub seams. Shape with the shaping tool. Wipe up excess with paper toweling.
11. Wait two hours for the caulk to set before draining tub.

You're done! Wait 12 hours (overnight) before using the tub.

93 Brick grout repair made easy

Replacing loose, damaged or missing mortar is very important. Make certain that you inspect all the brick on your house every spring and fall.

Remember the most important brick on your home is the chimney. If you can't see your chimney brick clearly, get a pair of binoculars and inspect them from the sidewalk so you can get a good angle.

Loose mortar on chimney brick may be symptom of a far more serious problem. Moisture may have gotten into the chimney and started degregating the interior brick. When that happens it can cause the entire chimney to have to be replaced.

You probably don't belong on the top of the roof trying to do cement work and hold on at the same time. If you see loose mortar, seriously consider calling in a professional chimney cleaning company or ask a masonry supply company for a referral for someone to re-point the chimney and do an interior chimney brick inspection. This is very important. Don't procrastinate, call in the experts.

If the loose or missing mortar around brickwork is close enough to the ground for safety, you can easily do it yourself. Gibraltar and other companies have come out with tubes of mortar grout material that make easier and more user friendly than ever.

Shopping List: Tubes of Gibraltar Mortar Repair or bags of Mason Mix, garden hose, plugging or joining chisel and bricklayers hammer, goggles, gloves, whiskbroom, caulk gun, mortar trowel, jointer or piece of dowel rod.

Directions:
1. Spray down the entire brick area with a garden hose. This both helps clean the area and dampens the surrounding brick so that it will not draw moisture from the new mortar.

2. Clear all the old loose mortar from the joint between the bricks. You may need to use a cold chisel and hammer to get some of the damaged mortar out.
3. Chisel out the damaged mortar joint to a depth of at least one-half inch. When doing this be sure to wear goggles.
4. Clean out the joint by blowing or brushing away with a whiskbroom.
5. Fill in the joint with mortar mix. The easiest way to do this is with a tube of Gibraltar Mortar Repair in a standard caulking gun. The square applicator tip is designed for mortar joints.

If you can't find the tube of Mortar Repair you will have to do it the old fashioned way. Mix up a very small batch of mason mix. Use only a little water. The mixed mortar should be a plastic-like consistency.

Photo courtesy of Quikrete

Put the mixed mortar on a small board that you will use as your pallet. Using the bottom edge of a mortar trowel, pick up a small amount of the mortar and carefully push it into the cracks. Be careful not to get the mortar on the surrounding brickwork.

6. When you've done a few bricks and the mortar is thumb-print hard, finish off the joints by drawing a jointer or piece of dowel rod across each mortar joint at a 45 degree angle to match the old mortar joint. Make sure you do this after you have finished each area.

7. If an entire brick has become loose, take out the entire brick and chisel away all mortar. Then butter the top, bottom and sides of the brick with mortar and push it into place. Remove excess mortar immediately and finish off the joints as soon as the mortar gets thumbprint hard.

94 How to maintain and repair concrete drives and walks

The three most common homeowner concrete problems are spalling, cracking and heaving. We'll tackle them in consecutive order

Spalling:
Spalling is a condition in which a relatively large but shallow surface area has lost its cohesive quality and exposed the aggregate. If there is just a limited amount of spalling you will probably fix each exposed area separately. If the damage is wide-spread you will probably want to consider re-surfacing the concrete.

Small area:
Clean away all broken and loose concrete, dirt and plant remains. If a large area has to be repaired, pressure-wash the surface a few days beforehand. Dirt and grease stains can be removed with Quikrete Concrete and Asphalt Cleaner or a mixture of four ounces dry measure of Trisodium Phosphate (TSP) per gallon of water.

Photo courtesy of Quikrete

Resurface the area with Quikrete Vinyl Concrete Patcher. This product is a blend of vinyl resin, fine sand and Portland Cement. It has very strong adhesive properties and can be troweled to a 1/16-inch feather edge.

Do not mix more than you can use in a half-hour because it becomes unworkable after that period of time.

256

If the area being repaired only has to be built up 1-inch or less you can do the job in one application. If you need more than one inch, it should be done in two or more applications. Allow the product to cure for a couple of days between applications.

Large Area

If you have a large weathered and pockmarked area you can resurface the entire area to look like new rather easily thanks to a new Quikrete product called Quikrete Concrete Resurfacer. I am being very specific about the product because, as far as I know, it is unique and you just won't find it by anyone else. Concrete Resurfacer is a special blend of Portland cement, sand, polymer modifiers and other additives. It doesn't shrink, can be applied very thin and wears extremely well.

The maximum area that can be repaired at any one time is 144 square feet (12' x 12').

Shopping List: Quikrete Concrete Resurfacer, very powerful power washer capable of 3,500 psi, garden hose, duct tape or weather stripping, steel finishing trowel, large industrial squeegee, wall paper brush, push broom, heavy duty drill with paddle mixer, 5 gallon mixing bucket, hammer, chisel, gloves, safety goggles, broom.

Directions:

1. The entire area must be meticulously cleaned with the power washer. Unless you plan on going into the business you wouldn't want to own one of these things. It is so powerful that it is dangerous.

Photo courtesy of Quikrete

257

When working make sure that kids, dogs and bystanders are out of the way. Be sure to wear your goggles and gloves.

2. Divide the area into 12' X 12' sections and protect expansion joints with weather stripping or duct tape.

3. Level spalled areas and pock marks with a thick mix of 1 part water and 7 parts Concrete Resurfacer. Trowel into place and allow to dry before going to the next step.

4. Mix Concrete Resurfacer in the 5 gallon pail using the heavy duty drill and paddle mixer. The proportions are 7 pints of water per 40 pound bag of Concrete Resurfacer. If the mix is a little too thick add a little more water.

Quikrete Concrete Resurfacer can be used as long as the temperature is above 50° F for at least a 24 hour period. In cold weather it is best to use 120° (hot) water. In hot weather use cold water and work only in the shade or the coolest parts of the day.

5. Saturate surface with water and remove standing water.

6. Pour concrete mix on surface and spread out with the long handled squeegee. Really scrub the mix into the surface with the squeegee. Finish off hard to reach areas with the wall paper brush.

7. Within 5 minutes sweep the surface with a push broom to provide a professional looking surface. Push broom in one direction only across the entire surface.

Alternatively the surface could be smoothed with a trowel or the surface could be textured with the broom.

8. Let the newly resurfaced concrete pad stand for at least 24 hours before use.

9. Fill expansion joints following the directions on crack filling.

Cracks

Fill thin cracks less than 1/2-inch in width with a ready to use crack sealer. Just snip the top and pour. The crack sealer acts like an expansion joint. Many crack sealers or fillers are black like traditional expansion joints. Alcoguard is considered one of the best of these.

If you don't want the black lines, both Quikrete and American Stone Mix make gray concrete crack sealers. Pecora Corporation makes an excellent limestone colored sealant in 1 quart tubes that makes doing the job very easy. You can also use caulk tubes of Mortar Repair.

Cracks 1/2" thick or wider
When the cracks are 1/2-inch or wider, water will have washed a channel under the concrete.

Shopping List: play sand, backer rod sized to fit crack, crack sealer of your choice, ice chopper.

Directions:
1. Clean crack of debris.
2. Back fill these with play sand and tamp down with an ice chopper. Repeat the process several times.
3. When you have filled the crack until it is 1 1/2" from the top, stuff a backer rod that is slightly thicker than the crack is wide. You want a snug fit.
4. Pour or squeeze crack sealer into the crack.

Concrete heaving

When concrete cracks and is not repaired right away water seeps down the crack and washes away the sand and other ground under the concrete.

During the winter water from melting ice flows into the miniature cavern that is being formed under the concrete. Alternating freeze and thaw cycles keep lifting and dropping the concrete until one portion of the concrete has dropped one or more inches below the surface of the surrounding area

The job costs about 1/3 the price of new concrete so it is a money saver. When the job is done make certain that you treat all the expansion joints like 1/2" cracks and fill them with backer rod topped by crack sealer.

95 How to maintain and repair asphalt drives

Asphalt drives are popular because they are relatively inexpensive, long lasting and require little care. The biggest problem with asphalt is that we don't use it enough. Asphalt is like chewing gum. It stays supple as long as you chew. When you stop chewing it grows increasingly hard. Left alone for a long enough period of time and it become brittle.

The best thing we could do for an asphalt drive would be to drive over every section of it continuously. I don't mean just the tire groves, I mean the entire surface so that every square inch of drive would bounce up and down a couple of times a day.

If we did that the drive would never have to be sealed. Since we do not use the drives enough we seal the surface in an attempt to keep the outer surface from losing its oils and flexibility.

Sealing
Every year thousands of gallons of asphalt sealer will be applied for the wrong reason by well meaning Do-It-Yourselfers. Many people apply sealer every year as a beautifying agent. They like the deep, rich black color. Over time the sealer builds up and causes reflective cracking. If you apply a good quality sealer, you only have to re-apply it every two to four years.

Here are a few tips: Not all asphalt sealers are created equal. A good product will come in a Cold Tar formula and be fortified with sand for slip resistance and wearability.

Asphalt is weather sensitive. Pick a day when there will be no rain for 24 hours after the repair is completed.

Chuckholes

The secret to a long lasting patch is to have the chuckhole clean and dry before you start. Many asphalt companies make a couple of different kinds of asphalt sealer. One is for retail, the other for commercial use. You are better off getting the good stuff.

The premium product will be a lot more forgiving, can be applied in any weather. Sometimes there can even be water in the hole. Pour the patching material directly from the bag into

Photo courtesy of Quikrete

the hole. Over-fill so that there is a nice little mound. Then either tamp down by hand or drive over the mound with your car or truck. You're done.

Smaller Cracks

If the width of the crack is 2 inches or more, treat it like a chuckhole. A narrower crack can be fixed using pourable crack filler. Be sure that the crack is clean and dry with no vegetation before you begin.

There are three different types of crack filler: Asphalt Emulsion, Elastromeric, and Acrylic Crack Sealant. The Asphalt Emulsion is the least expensive.

An Elastromeric crack sealer, like Owens Corning TruGuard, costs $10 to $13 a gallon. It can cause a slight irritation if too much of it gets on your hands, but it lasts twice as long as an Asphalt Emulsion. Acrylic Crack Sealant can last slightly longer than Elastomerics and costs about $16 a gallon.

Dalton Enterprises has developed a product called Latex·ite Pli-Stix Permanent Crack Filler that gives the quality of a hot tar patch without any mess. Pli-Stix come in boxes of 1/2-inch width. The same product comes in a 150 foot, 2 gallon pail and is called Crack Stix.

To repair a crack, just break off a length of the proper width Pli-Stix and stuff it into the crack. If a crack is a little too narrow for the 1/2-inch Pli-Stix, push in the 1/2-inch. Then Melt the Pli-Stix with a Bernz-O-Matic torch. As soon as the product has melted, you're done.

If the crack is deep, fill with play sand to within 1/4-inch of the top. Tamp down the sand with an ice chopper, and then over-fill with your choice of crack sealer.

96 Proper lubrication will make your garage door last longer

As soon as the weather gets cold, many garage doors moan and groan when raised or lowered. That noise is a sign of improper lubrication or alignment and could take years off the life of the door.

Clean first, then lubricate
There are two steps to lubricating a garage door. First, the old grease and gunk has to be removed; then the hinges and moving parts should be oiled. I prefer to use white lithium grease on the door pin hinges and 3-in-One Oil or Tri-Flow spray on other moving parts.

Taking the old gunk off is more important than applying the new lubricant. Once it turns cold, old grease build-up pulls at moving parts and causes premature door failure. Spray WD-40 everywhere there is old, sticky grease. Then remove the mess with paper towels.

It is especially important to clean roller guide tracks and other places that should not really have been greased. If your garage has an older Stanley Door with a tube-type door opener, spray the tube with WD-40 and remove grease buildup with paper towels. Once the grease is removed, lightly lubricate all moving parts with 3-in One-Oil.

Different garage doors have different lubrication points
There are basically two different types of garage doors — old-fashioned tilt-out doors and sectional doors. On old tilt-out doors

be sure to lubricate the pivot points where the arms connect to the wall. There are two door pivots, left and right. Also lubricate the roller where the arm connects to the door and where the spring connects to the arm.

On sectional doors, lubricate the overhead torsion springs, rollers, hinges and anything that moves. Do not accidentally lubricate roller tracks. The tracks should be kept clean and dry, so that rollers move back and forth effortlessly.

Keep door tracks lubricant free
When it comes to lubricating door opener systems, do not lubricate the track or the tube on the door openers. Lubricating these parts makes them so sticky that movement becomes almost impossible during cold weather.

Check the manual that came with your garage door opener before lubricating the chain or tracks on the door opener. On some models, grease buildup can cause such problems that lubrication is forbidden. On the other hand, some screw drive openers need to be lubricated to function properly.

Replace weather stripping at bottom of door
Garage door weather stripping wears away because it rubs against the concrete every time you close the door. Replace it whenever it gets worn or wind, water, leaves and snow can blow in.

97 Clean and lubricate all doors and locks once a year

Winter is the worst season of the year for door and lock failure because the oil and grease that lubricates them gets very sticky and tugs on all moving parts.

The best defense is to give every moving part of your doors a thorough cleaning and lubrication before the onset of winter.

White lithium grease is weather resistant

It is very important to choose the proper lubricating agent to do the job. There is a big difference between lubricants and grease. Lubricants are usually thin liquids that reduce friction between metal parts. Grease acts like a cushion between metal parts. White lithium grease is very weather resistant and stays on the metal no matter what the temperature or weather condition.

Entrance doors

Treat the hinges on exterior and storm doors with a squirt of 3-in-One oil. If you see traces of black grease take the door off the hinges and clean the door pins and hinges thoroughly before spraying lithium grease on the pins and put the door back up.

WD-40 makes an excellent metal cleaner. You could spray WD-40 on hinge pins or any greasy metal part to cut through old grease. After the WD-40 cuts through the old grease, wipe it off and apply the proper lubricant.

Locks should be dusted with graphite. If they don't work effortlessly now, they will be a problem this winter. Squirt WD-40 into the keyhole and let it dry for a few minutes.

When the lock is dry, puff in powdered graphite.

Upgrade door sweep to brush-style
Check the door sweep at the bottom of each entrance door. It may have worn away or changed shape. If it shows wear or is no longer flexible replace it with the original equipment, or a brush-style sweep.

Sliding glass door walls
The rollers on sliding glass doors see heavy action. Clean the lower guide thoroughly. Wipe old grease off rollers with a rag dampened with mineral spirits or denatured alcohol. Lubricate with 3-in-One oil or white lithium grease.

98   How to lower basement humidity

Even a waterproofed basement can be humid if it is not properly insulated. Cool basement walls can cause condensation when the inside air is relatively warm and humid.

You can solve the problem three ways.

1.   The first and least expensive is to use a dehumidifier and fan combination. Put the dehumidifier at one side of the room and the fan on the other. Direct the fan to blow at the ceiling about mid-way between the two. Put the fan on a timer, 6 hours on, 2 hours off. The fan/dehumidifier combo make the dehumidifier at least 50% more efficient. The fan costs only a few pennies a day to run. This should do the trick for most basements.

2.   You can install a super dehumidifier like the Santa Fe by Therma-Stor LLC. The Santa Fe is like a residential dehu-

midifier on steroids. It can remove over 100 pints of water per day. The unit is also ultra-efficient, removing two to three times more water for the same cost as operating a standard residential dehumidifier.

3.   The nicest way to make a finished basement dry and cozy is to install a natural gas direct vent fireplace. Dry warmth eliminates humidity while the dancing flames add charm.

99   How to stop floors from squeaking

Your floors may be trying to tell you something important. If they squeak during the winter but not during the summer they are telling you that there is not enough humidity in the house. Increase the humidity to the proper seasonally adjusted level and the squeaks will go away in about 30 days.

If the squeaks are happening all the time you need some other fixes.

Hardwood flooring
Spray some powdered graphite between the boards where the tongue and groove connects.

First floor fixes
The best way to fix a floor is often from the floor below, i.e. the basement. These fixes are two person jobs. One person walks on the floor and locates the squeak; the other person fixes the problem from the floor below.

Shims
Get a bundle of shims and some silicone spray from the hardware store. Once the squeak is located spray silicone on a shim and pound the shim between the joist immediately under the squeak

and the sub floor. If the squeak is still there pound another shim in next to the one you have already placed.

If this fixes the problem, you are a hero, go on to the next squeak. If the shims didn't solve the problem, it is time for the heavy artillery.

Kant-Sag Straps or Squeak-Enders
Kant-Sag Straps by USP Structural Connectors, www.uspconnectors.com, pull the offending sub floor down to the joist and keeps it from moving thus eliminating the squeak.

Squeak Enders by E. & E. Engineering screw into the sub floor and pulls the sub floor and joist tight together.

Carpeted flooring
Carpeted flooring can be a problem. A special product, the Squeeeeek No More, was developed by O' Berry Enterprises, Inc..

The Squeeeeek No More kit includes a jig and special screws that break off under the carpeting. To stop the squeak you screw a unique two headed screw through the carpet, through the flooring and into the joist below. This pulls the sub floor snug against the joist and should eliminate the squeak. Then you snap off the upper head and shank so the screw is hidden from view.

100 If you know how long something should last, you will know when to shop

When most of us buy a house, or something for the house, we expect to last forever. That is usually unrealistic. On the opposite extreme other people discard products that aren't even teenagers yet just because they are bored. Still others of us are "shoppers" we see a great value on something and we want to buy because it is such a great value.

I thought it might help you in your decision making process to know what the accepted standard is for the service life of various appliances and home components. If something has outlived its recommended service life when it wears out, great, you are ahead of the game.

If something is almost at the end of its service live when we see a bargain, it just might make sense to replace it.

If we see a tremendous value on an appliance, but we see that our present one should last for five more years, maybe it is not time to make the move.

If something is falling apart and should still be going strong, bummer! Don't go to that store or buy that brand again.

To help with this mighty undertaking the U.S. Department of Housing and Urban Development's published Residential Rehabilitation Inspection Guide, 2000. Appendix C – Life Expectancy of

Housing Components gives industry standards for most of the components and appliances that are in the average house.

The writers listed the following caveat:

"The following material was developed for the National Association of Home Builders (NAHB) Economics Department based on a survey of manufacturers, trade associations and product researchers. Many factors affect the life expectancy of housing components and need to be considered when making replacement decisions, *including the quality of the components, the quality of their installation, their level of maintenance, weather and climatic conditions, and intensity of their use.*"

"Some components remain functional but become obsolete because of changing styles and tastes or because of product improvements. Note that the following life expectancy estimates are provided largely by the industries or manufacturers that make and sell the components listed."

Life Expectancy of Household Components

Appliances*	Life in years
Compactors	10
Dishwashers	10
Dryers	14
Disposal	10
Freezers, compact	12
Freezers, standard	16
Microwave ovens	11
Electric ranges	17
Gas ranges	19
Gas ovens	14
Refrigerators, compact	14
Refrigerators, standard	17
Washers, automatic and compact	13

Exhaust fans	20

*Source: Appliance Statistical Review, April 1990

Bathrooms*	**Life in years**
Cast iron bathtubs	50
Fiberglass bathtub and showers	10-15
Shower doors, average quality	25
Toilets	50

*Sources: Neil Kelly Designers, Thompson House of Kitchens and Bath

Cabinetry*	**Life in years**
Kitchen cabinets	15-20
Medicine cabinets and bath vanities	20

*Sources: Kitchen Cabinet Manufacturers Association, Neil Kelly Designers

Closet systems*	**Life in years**
Closet shelves	Lifetime

Countertops*	**Life in years**
Laminate	10-15
Ceramic tile, high-grade installation	Lifetime
Wood/butcher block	20+
Granite	20+

*Sources: AFP Associates of Western Plastics, Ceramic Tile Institute of America

Doors*	**Life in years**
Screen	25-50
Interior, hollow core Less than	30
Interior, solid core	30-lifetime

Exterior, protected overhang	80-100
Exterior, unprotected and exposed	25-30
Folding	30-lifetime
Garage doors	20-50
Garage door opener	10

*Sources: Wayne Dalton Corporation, National Wood Window and Door Association, Raynor Garage Doors

Electrical*   Life in years

Copper wiring, copper plated, copper clad aluminum, and bare copper	100+
Armored cable (BX)	Lifetime
Conduit	Lifetime

*Source: Jesse Aronstein, Engineering Consultant

Finishes used for waterproofing* Life in years

| Paint, plaster, and stucco | 3-5 |
| Sealer, silicone, and waxes | 1-5 |

*Source: Brick Institute of America Floors

Floors*   Life in years

Oak or pine	Lifetime
Slate flagstone	Lifetime
Vinyl sheet or tile	20-30
Terrazzo	Lifetime
Carpeting (depends on installation, amount of traffic, and quality of carpet)	11
Marble (depends on installation, thickness of marble, and amount of traffic)	Lifetime+

*Sources: Carpet and Rug Institute, Congoleum Corporation, Hardwood Plywood Manufacturers Association, Marble Institute, National Terrazzo and Mosaic Association, National Wood Flooring Association, Resilient Floor Covering Institute

Footings and foundation*	Life in years
Poured footings and foundations	200
Concrete block	100
Cement	50
Waterproofing, bituminous coating	10
Termite proofing (may have shorter life in damp climates)	5

*Source: WR Grace and Company

Heating, ventilation and air conditioning (HVAC)* Life in years

Central air conditioning unit (newer units should last longer)	15
Window unit	10
Air conditioner compressor	15
Humidifier	8
Electric water heater	14
Gas water heater (depends on type of water heater lining and quality of water)	11-13
Forced air furnaces, heat pump	15
Rooftop air conditioners	15
Boilers, hot water or steam (depends on quality of water)	30
Furnaces, gas- or oil-fired	18
Unit heaters, gas or electric	13
Radiant heaters, electric	10
Radiant heaters, hot water or steam	25
Baseboard systems	20

Diffusers, grilles, and registers	27
Induction and fan coil units	20
Dampers	20
Centrifugal fans	25
Axial fans	20
Ventilating roof-mounted fans	20
DX, water, and steam coils	20
Electric coils	15
Heat Exchangers, shell-and-tube	24
Molded insulation	20
Pumps, sump and well	10
Burners	21

Sources: Air Conditioning and Refrigeration Institute, Air Conditioning, Heating, and Refrigeration News, Air Movement and Control Association, American Gas Association, American Society of Gas Engineers, American Society of Heating, Refrigeration and Air-Conditioning Engineers, Inc., Safe Aire Incorporated

Home security appliances*	Life in years
Intrusion systems	14
Smoke detectors	12
Smoke/fire/intrusion systems	10

Insulation	Life in years
For foundations, roofs, ceilings, walls, and floors	Lifetime

Sources: Insulation Contractors Association of America, North American Insulation Manufacturers Association

Landscaping	Life in years
Wooden decks	15
Brick and concrete patios	24
Tennis courts	10
Concrete walks	24
Gravel walks	4

Asphalt driveways	10
Swimming pools	18
Sprinkler systems	12
Fences	12

*Sources: Associated Landscape Contractors of America, Irrigation Association

Masonry*   Life in years

Chimney, fireplace, and brick veneer	Lifetime
Brick and stone walls	100+
Stucco	Lifetime

*Sources: Brick Institute of America, Architectural Components, National Association of
Brick Distributors, National Stone Association

Millwork*   Life in years

| Stairs, trim | 50-100 |
| Disappearing stairs | 30-40 |

Paints and stains   Life in years

Exterior paint on wood, brick, and aluminum	7-10
Interior wall paint (depends on the acrylic content)	5-10
Interior trim and door paint	5-10
Wallpaper	7

*Sources: Finnaren and Haley, Glidden Company, The Wall Paper

Plumbing*   Life in years

| Waste piping, cast iron | 75-100 |
| Sinks, enamel steel | 5-10 |

Sinks, enamel cast iron	25-30
Sinks, china	25-30
Faucets, low quality	13-15
Faucets, high quality	15-20

*Sources: American Concrete Pipe Association, Cast Iron Soil and Pipe Institute, Neil Kelly Designers, Thompson House of Kitchens and Baths

Roofing*	Life in years
Asphalt and wood shingles and shakes	15-30
Tile (depends on quality of tile and climate)	50
Slate (depends on grade)	50-100
Sheet metal (depends on gauge of metal and quality of fastening and application)	20-50+
Built-up roofing, asphalt	12-25
Built-up roofing, coal and tar	12-30
Asphalt composition shingle	15-30
Asphalt overlag	25-35

*Source: National Roofing Contractors Association

Rough structure*	Life in years
Basement floor systems	Lifetime
Framing, exterior and interior walls	Lifetime

*Source: NAHB Research Foundation

Shutters*	Life in years
Wood, interior	Lifetime
Wood, exterior (depends on weather conditions)	4-5

Vinyl plastic, exterior	7-8
Aluminum, interior	35-50
Aluminum, exterior	3-5

*Sources: A.C. Shutters, Inc., Alcoa Building Products, American Heritage Shutters

Siding*	Life in years
Gutters and downspouts	30
Siding, wood (depends on maintenance)	10-100
Siding, steel	50-Lifetime
Siding, aluminum	20-50
Siding, vinyl	50

Sources: Alcoa Building Products, Alside, Inc., Vinyl Siding Institute

Walls and window treatments*	Life in years
Drywall and plaster	30-70
Ceramic tile, high grade installation	Lifetime

*Sources: Association of Wall and Ceiling Industries International, Ceramic Tile Institute of America

Windows*	Life in years
Window glazing	20
Wood casement	20-50
Aluminum and vinyl casement	20-30
Screen	25-50

*Sources: Best Built Products, Optimum Window Manufacturing, Safety Glazing Certification Council, Screen Manufacturers Association

Appendix A - INDOOR MOLD CHART*

Master Handyman Press, Inc. has produced this chart as a public service. It is not to be considered a definitive work or primer. The assemblers claim no scientific expertise. The sole purpose of this chart is to give the reader some awareness of interior molds so that they may go to the source material for further study.

<u>MOLDS</u>

Alternaria alternata
Where found: **Window sills, walls, carpets, textiles**
Symptoms: Produces a mycotoxin, tenuazonic acid and other toxic metabolites. Cause of extrinsic asthma, may develop pulmonary emphysema.

Asperfillus fumigatus
Where found: **House dust, potting soil**
Symptoms: Human pathogen. Affects those immune compromised. Causes both invasive and allergic aspergillosis (infection of tissues - may effect lungs, ear canal, skin or mucus membrane). Symptoms include weight loss, fever, chills and blood in urine.

Aspergillus versicolor
Where found: **Wood, wallpaper glue**
Symptoms: Produces sterigmatocystin mycotoxin and cyclopiaxonic acid. Can cause diarrhea and upset stomach, also necrosis (progressive cell death) of kidney and liver.

Aureobasidium pullulans
Where found: **On caulk and paint in wet rooms like bath and kitchen**
Symptoms: Appears as dark spots, This is a first wave fungi that helps break down Cell walls so fungi like Cladosporium herbarum can set about the decomposition process.

Chaetomium sp
Where found: **Paper, sheetrock, cellulose**
Symptoms: Destructive to paper and plastics. Can produce Acremonium like state. Reported allergenic.

Cladosporium herbarum
Where found: **Window sills, wood, textiles fiberglass duct liners**
Symptoms: According to Suzanne Gravesen's almost impossible to find book, *Microfungi*, CH is the most important fungal airway allergen, causing asthma and hay fever. Some skin lesions (chromoblastomycosis) are possible.

Cladosporium sphaerospermum
Where found: **Paint, textiles, plants, wallpaper, carpet, fiberglass**
Symptoms: Not listed

Epicoccum sp
Where found: **Plants, soil, textiles, paper products**
Symptoms: A common allergen

Fusarium sp
Where found: **Soil, humidifiers**
Symptoms: Can produce trichothecene (induce hemorrhaging in lungs and brain and damage to bone marrow due to DNA synthesis inhibitions) toxins which target circulatory, alimentary, skin and nervous systems. Can produce hemorrhagic syndrome characterized by nausea, vomiting, diarrhea, dermatitis and internal bleeding.

Geotrichum sp
Where found: **Paper, soil, water**
Symptoms: Geotrichum candidum (rare fungal infection of mouth and regulatory tract and digestive tract - rarely a problem) can cause secondary infection in association with Tuberculosis causing lesions of the skin, bronchi, mouth, lung and intestine.

Paecilomyces sp
Where found: **Soil, dust, humidifiers, air, wallpaper**
Symptoms: Linked to wood-trimmers disease and humidifier associated illnesses. Reported allergenic. Some strains can clause pneumonia. Turns wallpaper green.

Papulospora sp
Where found: **Soil, textiles, paper**
Symptoms: Not listed

Penicillium chrysogenum
Where found: **Bioindicator of moisture in building. Often found in chipboard and paint.**
Symptoms: Not listed

Penicillium commune
Where found: **Bioindicator of moisture in building**
Symptoms: Releases mycotoxins into air. Toxic effects not yet sufficiently studied according to Microfungi.

Penicillium expansum
Where found: **Bioindicator of moisture in building**
Symptoms: Secretes citrinin and patulin which effect white blood cells and effect immune defense according to Grevesen's book Microfungi.

Penicillium sp
Where found: **Wallpaper, behind and in paint Fiberglass duct insulation**
Symptoms: Reported allergenic to skin. Common cause of extrinsic asthma. Acute symptoms include edema and bronchiospasms. Chronic cases may develop pulmonary emphysema.

Rhodotorula sp
Where found: **Very common red yeast found in carpeting cooling coils and drain pans**
Symptoms: Reported allergenic. Has colonized terminally ill patients.

Scopularispsis sp
Where found: **Wallpaper covered with Paris green, house dust**
Symptoms: Associated with type III Allergy; most often associated with an occupational disease like farmers may get from handling moldy hay. Potentially pathogenic. It has the ability to convert inorganic nitrogen to organic nitrogen compounds. Decompose arsenic compounds, which allows it to grow on paint containing arsenic. Often feeds on wallpaper and carpet adhesives containing arsenic compounds. May have caused Napoleon's death from arsenic poisoning.

Stachybotrys chartarum AKA, **Stachybotrys atra** and **Stachybotrys alternans**
Where found: **Rare. Carpet, drywall, cellulose**
Symptoms: May produce trichothecene nycotoxin-Satratoxin H which is poisonous by inhalation. Toxins are present on fungal spores. Spores die readily after release but are still allergenic and toxigenic.

Trichoderma sp
Where found: **Other fungi, drywall, cellulose, unglazed ceramics**
Symptoms: Produces antibiotics which are toxic to humans. Reported to be allergenic.

Ulocladium sp.
Where found: **Dead plants, drywall, cellulose, textiles**
Symptoms: Adds to symptoms of people allergic to Alternaria alternata.

Wallemia sp
Where found: **Textiles**
Symptoms: Very slow growth. Prefers dry conditions. No known human side effects.

---

* Compiled and condensed from the Foundation of the Wall and Ceiling Industry report: "Mold: Cause, Effect and Response" and the University of Minnesota Dept. of Environmental Health and Safety fungus Glossary on their web site. Some additions from Microfungi by Gravesen, et al.

This should just be the beginning of your search. We spent hours with various dictionaries and could not find out what some of these words meant. For more information and great technical expertise consult:

- Foundation of the Wall and Ceiling Industry, AWCI web site (http://www.awci.org/)

- University of Minnesota Department of Environmental Health and Safety Fungus Glossary (www.dehs/iaq/fungus/glossary.html)

- Medical dictionary created by Dr. Graham Dark; published by the Dept. of Medical Oncology, University of Newcastle upon Tyne, (c) Copyright 1997-2002 - The CancerWEB Project. All Rights Reserved. (http://cancerweb.ncl.ac.uk/cgi-bin/omd?action=Home&query=)

- *Microfungi,* by Suzanne Gravesen, Jens C. Frisvad and Robert A. Samson, 1st Edition, 1st printing, 1994, Munskgaard, ISBN: 87-16-11436-1, (c) Copyright 1994 - Gravesen, Frisvad, Samson and Munksgaard

Appendix B -PHONE NUMBERS & WEB SITES

Company/Phone/Web	Product or Service
3M (888) 364-3577 www.3m.com	Filtrete Air Filters
Advanced Environmental Recycling Technologies, Inc. (800) 951-5117 www.choicedek.com	ChoiceDek
Ag-Co Products (800) 522-2426 www.ag-coproducts.com	Egress Window-Well System
Air Life Environmental (800) 916-7873 www.airlifeone.com	Dynamic air cleaner
AirPal: (954) 426-9211 www.airpalspectra.com	UV air purification
AllergyZone (800) 704-2111 www.allergyzone.com	MERV 12 filter
Amaircare (877) 839-3036 www.amaircare.com,	Air Wash HEPA filter
Amazon Products (800) 832-5645 www.enviro-magic.com.	Mildew Stain Away
American Standard (800) 442-1902 www.americanstandard-us.com	Bath products

Company/Phone/Web	Product or Service
Anchor Decking Systems, Inc., (888) 898-4990 www.durabledeck.com	Durable Deck
Andersen (800) 426-4261 www.andersenwindows.com	Wood windows
Aqua-Air Technologies, Inc., (800) 854-5126 www.envirosept.com/index.html	EnviroSept electronic air filters
Association of the Nonwoven Fabrics Industry (919) 233-1210 www.inda.org	Filter industry association
AY McDonald Manufacturing (877) 795-PUMP www.aymcdonald.com	Saginaw Guardian Pump
Basement Systems, Inc (800) 541-0487 www.basementsystems.com	Interior waterproofing
Bath Ease, Inc. (727) 786-2604 www.bathease.com	Assisted shower
Betco (888) GO BETCO www.betco.com	Push Enzyme cleaner
Big D Industries (800) 654-4752 www.bigdind.com	Enzym D Enzyme cleaner
Bilco Scape Well (800) 854-9724 www.bilco.com	Egress window well system

Company/Phone/Web	Product or Service
Broan-Nutone (800) 548-0790 www.broan.com	Guardian Plus HEPA filter
Bryant (800) 428-4326 www.bryant.com	Furnace & air conditioner
Budget Electric (800) 400-8941 www.budget-electric.com	Electrical contractor
C. Crane Company (800) 522-8863 www.ccrane.com	Electronics distributor
Chicago Faucet Company – a Geberit Company (800) 323 – 5060 www.pf-2.com	PF/2 Energizer
Commercial Lighting Design, Inc. (800) 774-5799 www.lumalier.com	Lumalier
Controlled Energy Corp (800) 642-3199 www.ControlledEnergy.com	Bosch Aqua Star tankless water heater
Cosella Doerken (888) 4 DELTA4 www.cosella-doerken.com	Delta-DL Dimpled Plastic Water Barrier
Coy Construction Inc. (248) 363-1050 www.coyconstruction.com	Basement remodeler
CPI Plastics (866) 342-5366 www.eonoutdoor.com	Eon decking

Company/Phone/Web	Product or Service
Dalton Enterprises (800) 851-5606 www.latexite.com	Latex·ite Pli-Stix Permanent Crack Filler
DAP (888) DAP TIPS www.dap.com	Stain Kill sealers
Davey (866) DAV-PUMP www.daveyusa.com	XP & HS water pressure pumps
Discount Air Compressor and Generator Company (248) 338-2255 www.gohonda.com	Multi-fuel generators
Don Silver CKD/NKBA (800) 900-4761 www.donsilvers.com.	"Kitchen Design with Cooking in Mind"
Dow Chemical (800) 441-4369 www.dow.com	Wallmate solid foam insulation
Drytronic Inc., (800) 497-0579 www.drytronicinc.com	Electro-Osmotic Pulse (EOP) System
E. & E. Engineering (800) 323-0982 www.squeakender.com	Squeak Enders
Eaglebrook Products (888) 733-2546 www.smartdeck.com	Durawood EX
EFV/Brasscraft (888) 669-7356 None known	Magne Flo Valve

Company/Phone/Web	Product or Service
Environmental Dynamics Group (609) 275-9660 www.dynamicaircleaners.com	Dynamic distributor
Environmental Water Service (800-371-PURE) None known	Water filtration service
EPA Indoor Air Quality **Information Clearinghouse** (800) 438-4318 www.epa.gov/iaq/iaqinfo.html	Air Quality information
Fairway Tile and Carpet (866) 211-5558 www.fairwaycarpet.com	Enviro Cushion reseller
Field Controls www.fieldcontrols.com	UV air purification
Foundation of the Wall **and Ceiling Industry** (703) 534-8300 www.awci.org	Industry association
Geothermal Heat Pump Consortium www.geoexchange.org	The Geothermal
Gerber (847) 675-6570 www.gerberonline.com	Bath products
Gibraltar National (800) 442-7258 www.quikrete.com	Quikrete
Great Bay Products (727) 727-7130 www.flologicfl.com	FloLogic system 2000

Company/Phone/Web	Product or Service
Green Tree Composites, LLC, (877) 666-2742 www.monarchdeck.com.	Monarch Decking
Grundfos Pumps (877) 987-7867 www.grundfos.com	Comfort recirculating pump
Hartford and Ratliff (800) 466-3110 None known	Water heating specialist
Health Chek, LLC (866) 234-7579 www.moldchek.net	Mold test kit
Honeywell (800) 345-6770 www.honeywell.com/yourhome/	Air quality controls & cleaning
Icynene (800) 946-7325 www.icynene.com	Spray foam insulation
Kohler (800) 456-4537 www.kohlerco.com	Bath products
Kolbe & Kolbe Millwork (800) 477-8656 www.kolbe-kolbe.com	Wood windows & doors
Kroy Building Products (800) 933-5769 www.kroybp.com	Vinyl Decking
Laing Thermotech (619) 575-7466 www.lainginc.com	Instant hot water recirculating pump

Company/Phone/Web	Product or Service
Lasco Bathware (800) 877-2005 www.lascobathware.com	Assisted shower
Lennox (800) 9-LENNOX www.lennox.com	Heating, cooling, air cleaning
M.A.G. Engineering & **Manufacturing, Inc.** (800) 624-9942 www.magsecurity.com	Lock reinforcers
Magna Industries (800) 969-3334 www.sandkleen.com	Sand & Kleen
Marvin Windows (800) 346-5128 www.marvin.com	Wood windows
MI Community Insurance Agency (800) 430-8070 www.michigancommunity.com	Insurance agency
Midwest Infrared (517) 547-5439 www.midwestinfrared.com	Infrared thermal scanning
Monroe Infrared Technologies (800) 221-0163 www.monroeinfrared.com	Infrared thermal scanning
Mr. Sponge (800) 491-4686 www.mrsponge.com	Rod hole kit
Nibco (800) 234-0227 www.nibco.com	Just Right recirculating pump

Company/Phone/Web	Product or Service
Nirvana Safe Haven www.nontoxic.com/air/index.html	AllerAir UV & HEPA filters
O' Berry Enterprises, Inc. (800) 459-8428 www.squeaknomore.com	Squeeeeek No More
Oak Ridge National Laboratory (865) 574-0022 www.ornl.gov	US Government testing lab
Owens Corning (800) 438-7465 www.owenscorning.com	Insullation & roofing
Owens Corning (800) GET- PINK www.owenscorning.com	Roofing, siding, insulation, windows
Pella (800) 847-3552 www.pella.com	Wood windows
Performance Coatings (800) 736-6346 www.penofin.com	Penofin
Pittsburgh Corning Glass Block (800) 624-2120 www.pittsburghcorning.com	Glass block
Precision Plumbing Products (503) 256-4010 www.pppinc.com	Water hammer arrestors
Pultronex Corporation (800) 990-3099 www.ezdeck.com	EZ Deck

Company/Phone/Web	Product or Service
Research Products (608) 257-8801 www.resprod.com	Aprilaire furnace humidifiers
Rinnai of America (800) 621-9419 www.rinnaina.com	Tankless water heater
Royal Crown Ltd. (800) 488-5245 www.royalcrownltd.com	Brock Deck
Rust-oleum (847) 367-7700 www.rustoleum.com	Tub & Tile Refinisher Epoxy Acrylic Paint
Sanit-Air (888) 778-7324 www.sanit-air.com	Air testing, duct cleaning and remediation
Second Wind (877) 263-9463 www.freshpureair.com	UV Photo-Catalytic Oxidation
Simer (800) 468-PUMP www.simerpump.com	Ace-in-the-Hole back up sump pump
Skuttle 848-9786 www.skuttle.com	Model 216 air makeup unit(800)
Sloan Flushmate (800) 875-9116 www.flushmate.com	Pressure toilet
St. James Company (800) 344-4849 None known	Composite windows

Company/Phone/Web	Product or Service
Sterling (800) STERLING www.sterlingplumbing.com	Bath products
Swan (314) 231-8148 www.theswancorp.com	Assisted shower
Taco, Inc. (401) 942-8000 www.wagsvalve.com	Wags Water heater Shut Off Valve
Tech Results Inc. (718) 268-7126 www.antiscald.com	Anti scald devices
Thermal Industries (800) 245-1540 www.thermalindustries.com	DreamDeck
Therma-Stor LLC (800) 533-7533 www.thermastor.com	Santa Fe Super Dehumidifier
Toto (888) 295-8134 www.totousa.com	Bath products
Traco (888) 292-7600 www.traco.com	Wood windows
Tremco Barrier Solutions, Inc. (800) DRY-BSMT www.guarenteeddrybasements.com	Tuff-N-DRI waterproofing system
Trex Company (800) 289-8739 www.trex.com	Composite decking

Company/Phone/Web	Product or Service
Tri Brothers Chemical Corp. (847) 564-2320 None known	Mag-Erad manufacture
Univ. of MN / Dept. **of Environmental Health** www.dehs.umn.edu/iaq/fungus	Safety Fungus Glossary
Versa Dek Industries (800) 497-3325 www.versadek.com	Versa Dek
Versatile Building Products (800) 535-3325 www.deckcoatings.com	Versa Deck – Plus
Wallside (800) 521-7800 www.wallside.com	Vinyl windows
Water Furnace Co., The (800) 222-5667 www.waterfurnace.com	Geothermal heat pump
Weather Shield (800) 477-6808 www.weathershield.com	Wood windows
Weathergard (800) 377-8886 www.weathergardwindow.com	Vinyl windows
WellCome Home Project (765) 285-1471 www.bsu.edu/wellcomehome	Universal design
West Michigan Glass Block (800) 766-0500 www.wmgb.com	Basement Egress Windows

Company/Phone/Web	Product or Service
Wingits grab bars (877) 8 WINGIT www.wingits.com	Grab bars
Wm. Zinsser (732) 469-4367 www.zinsser.com	Stain Kill sealers
X-10 (800) 675-3044 www.x10.com	X-10 technology supplier
Xavier (734) 462-1033 www.equaliz-air.com	Equaliz-Air air makeup unit
Xypex Chemical (888) 443-7922 www.xypex.com	HD-150 waterproofing coating
Zircon (800) 245-9265 www.zircon.com	Stud & electric circuit finders

---

"Guidelines on Assessment and Remediation of Fungi in Indoor Environments" by the New York City Department of Health & Mental Hygiene Bureau of Environmental & Occupational Disease Epidemiology, www.ci.nyc.ny.us/html/doh/html/epi/moldrpt1.html.

"RESIDENTIAL CONSTRUCTION PERFORMANCE GUIDELINES for Professional Builders & Remodelers – 2nd Edition", produced by the NAHB Remodelors Council and The Single Family Small Volume Builders Committee.

"Fighting Mold – The homeowners' Guide" by Canada Mortgage & Housing Corporation, www.cmhc-schl.gc.ca.

Medical dictionary created by Dr. Graham Dark; published by the Dept. of Medical Oncology, University of Newcastle upon Tyne, © Copyright 1997-2002 - The CancerWEB Project. All Rights Reserved, www.cancerweb.ncl.ac.uk/omd. NAHB bookstore, (800) 223-2665, or on the Web at www.builderbooks.com.

The Owens Corning US Department of Energy insulation recommendations for your zip code www.owenscorning.com/around/insulation/rvalue.asp then click on Building, renovating & maintaining >Self-Help and Problem Solving Moisture and Mold.

INDEX

purification systems, 181-183
shut off, 218
supply, upgrading, 179
tank replacement, 194-196
tank temperature, 192
tank test, 186
Tite Mold and Mildew-Proof
Waterproofing Paint, 82
trail, 223
hot, instant, 179-180
Wayne Pump submersible, 199
Weather Shield, 96
Weathergard, 96
Web sites, 296-309
West Michigan Glass Block, 81
Weyerhaeuser, 102
Whole house natural gas powered generator, 211
Whole house surge protectors,
208-209
Whole house water system,
181-183
Williams
Refrigeration and Heating, 140
Jim, 140
Wilsonart, 71
Window installation, quality, 95
Windows,
casement, 100
clad, 96
composite, 96
double hung, 99
fiberglass, 96
metal-framed, 96
sliders, 100
vinyl, 96
wood framed, 96

Wingits, 78
X-10 , 164
technology, 164-166
Xavier Equaliz-Air, 143
Xypex - HD 150, 80. 82
Yaun Co., 183
Zebra stripes, 142
Zinsser, Wm., 82
Zircon, 219
Zoeller, 199
Zoller .3 submersible, 199

Look for Glenn Haege's upcoming books:

HAEGE'S HOMESTYLE ARTICLES,
The Detroit News, 2002-2003, available February, 2004

GLENN HAEGE'S 100 MOST IMPORTANT PAINTING TIPS

and

GLENN HAEGE 100 MOST IMPORTANT CLEANING TIPS

Coming Spring/Summer 2004

For the latest information on Glenn Haege, his books, articles and radio show, as well as hundreds of How To and Home Improvement articles, click on the Master Handyman Press Help Site:
www.MasterHandyman.com.